DATE DUE

	OCT 6 '98		
	OCT 13 '98	1 6 98	

*12487

Thank you

Donated by the P.T.S.O.

1989

The
Virginia Colony

by Dennis B. Fradin

Consultants: Barbara Miller, M.A.
Leslie Hendrikson, M.A.
Social Science Education Consortium, Inc.

CHILDRENS PRESS®
CHICAGO

Acknowledgment

Special thanks to Nelson Lankford, Ph.D.
Virginia Historical Society

For her help, the author thanks:
Diana Judith Fradin

Library of Congress Cataloging in Publication Data

Fradin, Dennis B.
The Virginia Colony.

Includes index.
Summary: Presents the history, economy, culture, and people of the Virginia colony from the early Indian settlements to the Revolution. Includes brief biographies of prominent Virginians of the period from Powhatan to Thomas Jefferson and Henry Lee.
1. Virginia—History—Colonial period, ca. 1600-1775—Juvenile literature.
2. Virginia—History—Revolution, 1775-1783—Juvenile literature.
[1. Virginia—History—Colonial period, ca. 1600-1775. 2. Virginia—History—Revolution, 1775-1783] I. Title.
F229.F755   1986   975.5'02   86-13639
ISBN 0-516-00387-9

Table of Contents

From left to right, *Godspeed*, *Susan Constant*, and *Discovery* approach Virginia for the first time.

Chapter I

The Original Virginians

Captain Smith, some doubt I have of your coming hither, that makes me not so kindly seek to [help] you as I would. For many do inform me your coming is not for trade, but to invade my people and possess my country.

Chief Powhatan to John Smith, 1609

At four o'clock on the morning of April 26, 1607, three small ships, carrying about one hundred Englishmen, neared the coast of what is now southeastern Virginia. After more than four months at sea, the Englishmen were happy to see land. Their excitement grew as the rising sun shone on the lovely forests and meadows of the Virginia seashore.

The Englishmen sailed up a river that they named James after their king, James I of England. From time to time, the men left their ships. They were looking for a good place to build a colony. As they did so, they were watched by a people who would later be both friend and foe of the colony. These people were the Indians, and we

King James I (1566-1625) from a painting by Paul Vansomer

5

Drawing from a copper engraving by De Bry, showing Virginia Indians fishing from a canoe

must begin our story of the Virginia Colony with them.

Before the Europeans came, many tribes of Indians lived in what is now the state of Virginia. The Powhatan* and the Susquehanna were two tribes that lived along the coast. The Monacan and Manahoac were two that lived in Virginia's central plain. The Cherokee lived with other tribes in the mountains and valleys of what is now western Virginia.

Most Indians lived in villages near sparkling blue rivers. Many cities and towns of modern-day Virginia were built on or very close to the sites of old Indian villages.

* For more information about Powhatan, chief of the Powhatans, see page 16

Present-day City or Town	Indian Village on or near that Site	Tribe
Alexandria	As-sa-o-meck	Powhatan
Cape Charles	Ac-cow-mack	Powhatan
Charlottesville	Monasukapanough	Monacan
Columbia	Rassawek	Monacan
Fredericksburg	Sock-o-beck	Powhatan
Goochland	Massinacack	Monacan
Hampton	Ke-cough-tan	Powhatan
Norfolk	Ski-co-ak	Powhatan
Petersburg	Ap-pa-ma-tuck	Powhatan
Richmond	Powhatan	Powhatan
Suffolk	Man-tough-que-me-o	Powhatan

The first known drawings of North American Indians

By looking at maps drawn by John Smith and other early European explorers, historians have been able to draw their own maps showing the location of Indian villages in relation to some present-day Virginia cities.

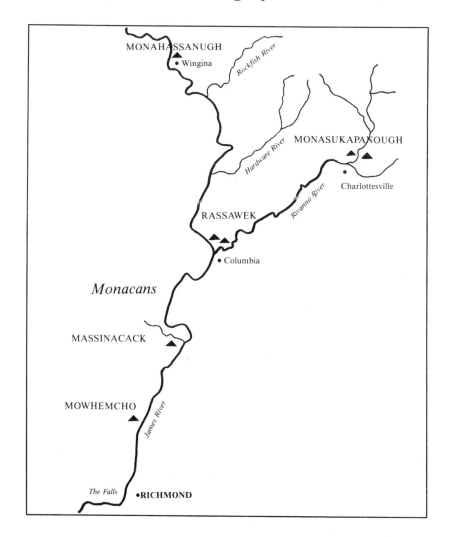

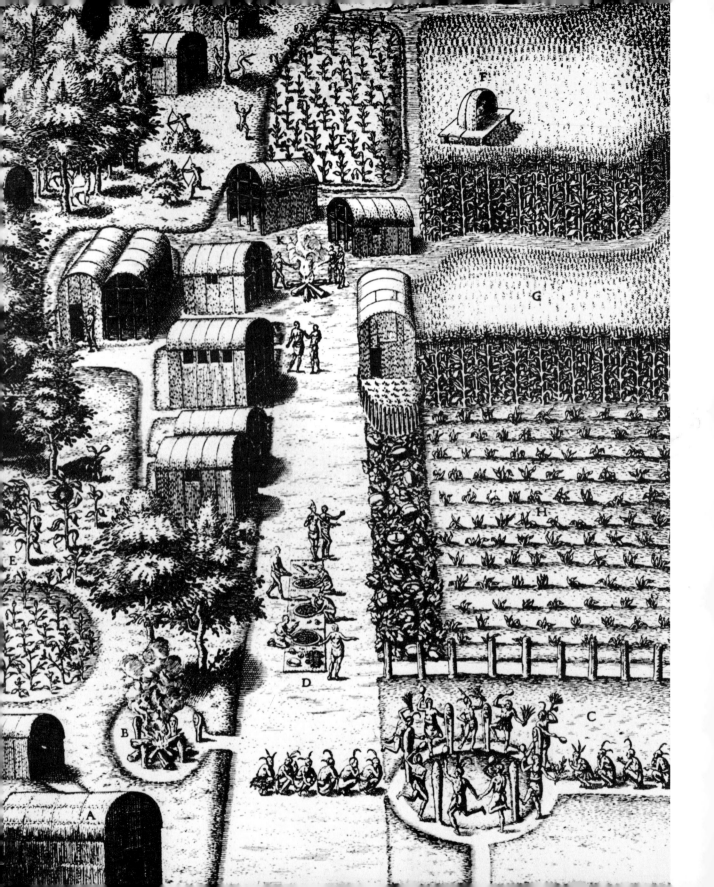

Each village was home to between several hundred and a thousand people. They lived either in dome-shaped cabins called wigwams or in large, oblong structures called longhouses. The walls of both types of homes were made out of young trees and had roofs made of tree bark. For protection, many of the villages were surrounded by palisades—walls of tall wooden posts.

Inside each dwelling lived a family which might include a husband, wife, and children and perhaps also aunts, uncles, cousins, and grandparents. One of the first Virginia colonists, Captain John Smith,* described how the Indians divided up their work among the men, women, and children:

> The men bestow their times in fishing, hunting, wars, and such man-like exercises, scorning to be seen in any woman-like exercise, which is the cause that the women be very painful [exhausted], and the men often idle. The women and children do the rest of the work. They make mats, baskets, pots, mortars, pound their corn, make their bread, prepare their victuals, plant their corn, gather their corn, bear all kind of burdens, and such like.

Each village had land for farming. Here the women and children grew not only corn, as Captain Smith mentioned, but also beans, pumpkins, melons, and tobacco.

* For more information about John Smith see page 17

(Opposite page): Drawing, based on John White's 1585 sketches, shows typical Indian village. Longhouses (A), ceremonial fires (B), cornfields (F and G), and eating areas (D) are clearly shown.

Romantic version of a young Indian admiring a maize (corn) plant after a painting by Frederick Remington

Indians hunted with bows and arrows.

While the women and children farmed, the men usually fished or hunted for food. They fished with nets, with poles equipped with bone hooks, or with spears. Sometimes they even lassoed sturgeon, a large fish, with ropes!

Virginia was home to large numbers of deer, elk, bears, wild turkeys, and bison, all of which the men hunted. Generally, dozens of hunters would go out together, surround their prey, and then set fire to the grass and brush in a large circle. The trapped and half-smothered animals would then make easy targets for the hunters' arrows.

The Indians used almost every part of the animals they killed. They made clothes and moccasins out of the skins, and sewing needles and fishing hooks out of the bones. Deer horns were used to make glue. Bird feathers were used in headdresses. The most important use of the animals, however, was as food.

The women cooked the meat, fish, and vegetables. They baked bread out of corn, wild oats, or sunflower seeds. The women also cooked a

Indians raised corn and gathered nuts and berries.

Indians cooking fish

variety of soups, including a very tasty one made
with oysters and mussels. At mealtime the family
would sit on grass mats and eat with their hands
or with wooden spoons.

On holidays, or when they had something
special to celebrate, the villagers would build a
large bonfire and gather around it. Music was

important during such celebrations. Shaking their gourd rattles, blowing on their reed flutes, and pounding on their drums, the Indians would sing, dance, and tell stories of their tribe's achievements.

Games were played at these festivals. The Indians set up wooden goalposts and played a kind of soccer game with a deerskin ball. They also played a stickball game which was much like lacrosse. They held contests to see who could shoot their arrows most accurately at a target.

Indian peace pipe

Prayer was a vital part of Indian celebrations and an important part of daily life as well. Like the ancient Greeks and Romans, the Indians worshiped many gods. They believed in gods of the sun, the wind and other forces of nature.

The Powhatan tribe thought the Great Hare created Earth and everything on it. They believed that Powhatans who died went up to the top of a very high tree. From there they took a path that led to the palace of the Great Hare, who lived near the rising sun. When the spirits finally arrived at the god's dwelling place, they went out into a lovely field. Here they did nothing but sing, dance, and feed on delicious fruits with the Great Hare

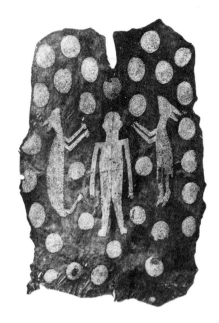

Powhatan's mantle. The figures on either side of the human form might represent the Great Hare.

and their own ancestors. The Powhatan believed that the departed spirits lived with the Great Hare until they became old. Then they would die and be born again on Earth.

Indian children did not go to school. They learned by observing and listening to their elders. From the tribe's songs and stories, they learned their people's history and religious beliefs. They learned to count by making notches on a stick, to tell the hour of the day by watching the sun, and to keep track of the time of month by looking at the cycles of the moon. Working alongside their elders, children learned to hunt, cook, farm, and make canoes. They were also taught the traditional Indian values. These included patience, persistence, the ability to endure hardship, and love toward one's friends and kin.

Their way of fighting war was one important way that the Indians differed from the one hundred or so men who came up the river in 1607. The Europeans had rules about how to fight a war. They thought that it was cowardly to make a sudden (or "sneak") attack. The Indians fought like hunters. Instead of charging up hills to fight their enemies, they hid behind the hills and attacked when their opponents least expected it.

Another important way that the Indians differed from the Europeans had to do with land. To the Indians land was like the sky—something you could enjoy but not own. The Europeans believed that land could be owned just as one owned a gun or a bag of beads. The Europeans desire to own the Indians' homeland was the main reason that the two groups would often clash.

Indian club

POWHATAN (About 1547-1618)

It is thought that Wahunsonacock (later known as Powhatan) was born in the Florida area in about 1547. When Wahunsonacock was young, Spanish explorers and conquerors arrived in his homeland and drove the Indians out. Wahunsonacock moved with his people northward to Virginia, where his father conquered half a dozen tribes and made them the confederacy known as the Powhatan tribe.

When he reached adulthood, Wahunsonacock inherited the chieftainship from his father, then conquered more tribes. By the time English colonists arrived, Wahunsonacock ruled thirty tribes of about ten thousand people who lived in more than one hundred villages in Tidewater Virginia. Because the Indians believed that to say one's real name aloud was unlucky, Wahunsonacock was called Powhatan. This was also the name of his people and of his favorite village, which stood on the James River near modern-day Richmond, Virginia. Powhatan spent much of his time in this village with his several wives and his numerous children, including his favorite, Pocahontas.

Powhatan was described as a harsh ruler by John Smith, who painted this word picture of him:

> He is of personage a tall, well proportioned man, with a sour look, his head somewhat gray, his beard so thin, that it seemeth none at all, his age near sixty; of a very able and hardy body to endure any labor. About his person ordinarily attendeth a guard of 40 or 50 of the tallest men his country doth afford. Every night upon the four quarters of his house are four sentinels.

From the beginning, Powhatan knew that the English had come to take his people's land. In a conversation with John Smith shortly after the Englishmen's arrival, Powhatan told him, "Many do inform me your coming is not for trade, but to invade my people and possess my country." In another talk, Smith invited Powhatan to Jamestown to receive presents sent by the English king. Sensing that the English might be planning to murder him or to trick him into accepting James as his king, Powhatan angrily responded:

> If your King has sent me presents, I also am a King, and this is my land. Eight days I will stay [here] to receive them. Your father [Christopher Newport, a leader of Jamestown] is to come to me, not I to him; nor yet to your fort. Neither will I bite at such a bait.

Powhatan used every tactic he knew to keep his country out of the hands of the English. When he traded corn to them, he tried to get some "thunder-sticks" in return. That tactic did not work, however, because

16

John Smith refused to trade guns to the Indians. During those times when the colonists were weakened by hunger and disease, Powhatan ordered his people to attack, but this did not drive the English away either.

One mystery surrounding Powhatan is why he allowed his daughter Pocahontas to marry the Englishman John Rolfe in 1614. Perhaps by this time the old chief realized that he could not beat the English and that a marriage between Rolfe and his favorite daughter would help keep the peace.

JOHN SMITH (1580-1631)

Born in the country village of Willoughby, England, John Smith as a boy loved to read about knights of the Middle Ages and wars in faraway lands. By comparison, his real life, which consisted of tending crops and livestock on the family farm and studying Latin and literature at school, seemed quite dull.

While still a boy, Smith sold his schoolbooks so that he would have enough money to run off to sea. His father discovered his plan and put an end to it. When Smith was sixteen, his father died and his mother remarried, leaving John on his own. Smith went to The Netherlands, where for three years he fought for the Dutch against the Spanish. At nineteen, he returned to England and went to live in a private woodland where he spent his time hunting deer, reading about warfare, and practicing his lancing skills on horseback.

After a short while in England, Smith went to Hungary to fight the Turks for the Hungarian army. In one battle he was wounded and then taken to Turkey as a slave. However, he killed his master, escaped, then made his way back to England by late 1604.

When the red-haired soldier with the piercing blue eyes heard that an expedition was being planned to settle Virginia, he joined it. He was largely responsible for the survival of Jamestown in its first years. Besides the famous meeting with Pocahontas, Smith had several other brushes with death while in Virginia. Once he was fishing in Chesapeake Bay when a stingray whipped its poisonous tail deep into his wrist. Certain that he would die, Smith had his companions dig a grave for him. He survived, however, and the stingray ended up as Smith's supper. The place where this happened is still known today as Stingray Point.

Despite his adventurous life, Smith found time to take notes about his experiences in Virginia. As a result, he made a map of Virginia that was used for nearly two centuries. Many of his observations about the Indians, climate, plants, and animals of Virginia were also used by later travelers.

After being injured in a gunpowder explosion in 1609, Smith returned to England. He had fallen in love with America, though, and wanted very much to return. He did so in 1614 when he explored the northeastern coast of what is now the United States. Captain Smith named this region New England and wrote a book about it called *A Description of New England.*

Smith offered his services to the Pilgrims who went to Massachusetts in 1620, but they said that *A Description of New England* was so good that they would use it as a guide and save the money they otherwise would have to pay him. Smith spent much of the remainder of his life writing about America and trying to encourage people to go there. Among his books were *The Generall Historie of Virginia, New England, and The Summer Isles,* and *The True Travels, Adventures, and Observations of Captaine John Smith, in Europe, Asia, Africa, and America.* John Smith, who escaped death so often that the Indians thought he was protected by special magic, died peacefully at the home of a friend in London at the age of fifty-one.

Cover of one of
John Smith's books

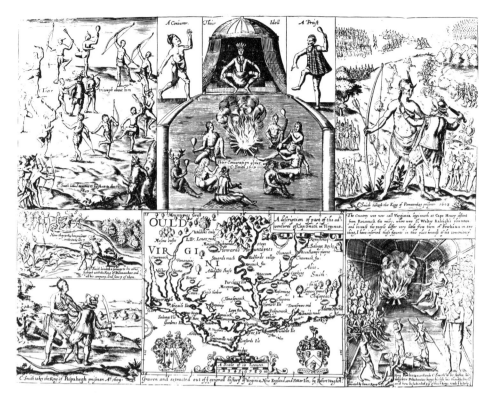

Graphic drawings (above) were used to dramatize Smith's adventures
in Virginia. Smith's maps (below) were descriptive and detailed.

Nineteenth-century drawing gives an idealized picture of the English landing at Jamestown.

Chapter II

Jamestown: First Permanent English Settlement in America

Within is a country that may have the prerogative [advantages] over the most pleasant places known, for large and pleasant navigable rivers, heaven and earth never agreed better to frame a place for man's habitation. . . . Here are mountains, hills, plains, valleys, rivers, brooks, all running most pleasantly into a fair bay, compassed but for the mouth, with fruitful and delightsome land. . . .

> *Captain John Smith, writing about Virginia in his 1624 book,* The Generall Historie of Virginia, New England, and the Summer Isles

As the three ships that were carrying the Englishmen sailed up the river that they called the James, some Indians who called the same river the Powhatan were watching them. It is possible that some of these Indians had seen Europeans before. In 1570, Spanish missionaries had built a settlement in Virginia that the Indians quickly destroyed. Later the English sent out

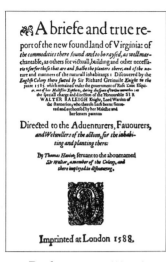

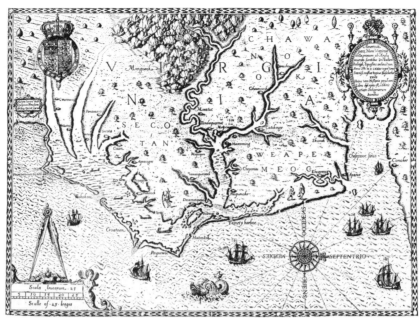

John White, who explored the coast of North America with Sir Walter Raleigh, drew this map in 1585.

Queen Elizabeth I
(1533-1603)

several ships to explore the coast of what is now the eastern United States. These explorers named this land Virginia, in honor of their Virgin Queen, Elizabeth I. However, the explorers of the late 1500s failed to set up any permanent settlements in Virginia or anywhere else in America.

The Indians watched from the forest as the Englishmen left their ships to explore. On one of their first landings, at a point that the English called Cape Henry, about thirty colonists were attacked by a small band of Indians. According to Captain John Smith, the Indians "hurt two of the English very dangerously."

To understand why the Indians attacked the English, it might help to reverse the situation. Pretend you lived in a village in England. What if, in the spring of 1607, a hundred Indian warriors with weapons arrived at your village and took land from you without asking permission? Would you fight?

To the Indians, the men who had arrived in the three "floating islands" and who were armed with "thunder-sticks" were invaders. They were the enemy.

With their different attitudes toward the ownership of land it was inevitable that the Indians and the English would fight.

Replicas of *Discovery* and *Godspeed* can be visited in restored Jamestown.

The three English ships—which were named the *Susan Constant,* the *Godspeed,* and the *Discovery*—continued up the James River for about sixty miles. Finally, on May 14, 1607, the colonists reached a small peninsula on the river's north side. They walked onto the marshy shore, looked around, and decided that this was a good place to build a fort. Here they could defend themselves from attack by either the Spanish or the Indians. They soon began work on their settlement, which they called Jamestown after King James I. Jamestown was to be the first permanent English settlement in America.

The colonists had been sent to Virginia by a group of wealthy London merchants called the Virginia Company of London. The London merchants hoped that the Virginia colonists would discover gold and other treasures, which they would ship back to England.

Unfortunately few of the first settlers of Jamestown were farmers or carpenters. They were accustomed to having others do this kind of work.

The seal of the Virginia Company of London, often called the London Company

The colonists had made the long and dangerous voyage across the Atlantic Ocean for many reasons. Because English laws at that time favored the oldest son, the younger children of wealthy families often inherited very little of their parents' land and possessions. Some of the colonists were younger sons who wanted land, which they could never have in their home country. Others were hungry for the gold that the London Company hoped would be found in Virginia. Still others wanted to introduce Christianity to the Indians. Finally, some were adventurers who were looking for excitement at the edge of the known world.

Before the ships had sailed, the names of the seven men who were to govern the colony were placed in a sealed box by the directors of the London Company. The box remained sealed until the men reached Virginia. When the box was opened, the colonists were not surprised by six of the names: Christopher Newport, the captain of the *Susan Constant*; Bartholomew Gosnold, captain of the *Godspeed*; John Ratcliffe, captain of the *Discovery*; John Martin, a sea captain who had once sailed with the great English explorer

Captain John Smith
(1580-1631) and his
coat of arms (right)

Sir Francis Drake; Edward Maria Wingfield, an investor in the London Company; and George Kendall, another sea captain. The seventh name, however, was a surprise. It belonged to a man who was neither a sea captain nor what the English thought to be a "gentleman." His name was John Smith, and he had spent most of the Atlantic voyage locked in irons after quarreling with Edward Wingfield.

The red-haired, blue-eyed, twenty-seven-year-old Smith had already lived through many adventures as a soldier of fortune in such places as The Netherlands, Hungary, and Romania. While fighting with the Hungarian army, Smith was wounded, then taken to Turkey as a slave. After escaping, he made his way back to England by late 1604. Growing restless after several years at home, Smith decided that the New World was the place for him to make his fame and fortune. He joined the London Company's Virginia expedition.

Despite the orders from the London Company, the other men on the governing council refused to admit John Smith. However, Smith soon proved that he was the man who was best able to help the colony survive.

Many of the Englishmen who came to Virginia were used to having servants do things for them. They were not very good at farming, working with their hands, or dealing with other people. Smith could do these things quite well. Smith also had the best military sense among the colonists.

In May of 1607, the governing council decided that about twenty men, including Smith, should explore the James River. Captain Smith protested that it was more important for the colonists to finish building the fort at Jamestown. They needed its protection. But the council ruled against Smith. Then, while he and the others were off exploring, Indians attacked the unfinished fort, killed two colonists, and wounded ten others. Several weeks after this tragic event, Smith was admitted to the governing council. He was soon recognized as the leader of the colony.

Under John Smith's direction the fort was completed by mid-June of 1607. Smith then had the men build the town's first thatch-roofed houses. Although the building went well, the colonists faced several big problems.

Everything in Jamestown has been reproduced to show visitors what the first permanent settlement in America looked like.

By the summer of 1607 the colony was running short of food. The Englishmen had planned to arrive in Virginia in time to plant crops, but the trip had taken longer than expected. It was too late to plant crops. The colonists tried to hunt and fish, but nearly all of them, except John Smith, were not able to do it. In the midst of a land full of wildlife and plant foods, the Jamestown colonists suffered from famine.

Disease was another terrible problem. Although the location of Jamestown was good for military reasons, it was very bad for health reasons. The drinking water was polluted, and the marshes near Jamestown were a breeding ground for mosquitoes. As a result, the colonists caught malaria, pneumonia, dysentery, and other diseases. By the end of the summer of 1607, almost half the Jamestown colonists were dead, and many more were dying.

From time to time the Indians came to the settlement with meat and corn, which they traded to the colonists for various trinkets. But the Englishmen could not get enough food from them. John Smith realized that, if any of the

John Smith trading with the Indians

Englishmen were to survive their first winter in Virginia, they would need to get large amounts of food from the Indians.

Smith led several food expeditions. Loaded down with mirrors, beads, and trinkets, Smith and a few other men would walk into an Indian village and bargain with them for deer meat, corn, and bread. Because the Indians did not trust the whites, these trading expeditions were quite dangerous.

In late December of 1607, John Smith was seeking food near the Chickahominy River when he and his little band were suddenly attacked by Powhatan Indians. Several of the colonists were killed, and Smith was taken prisoner.

Smith could tell that the Indians were thinking of killing him right away. To gain time, he pulled out his compass, and, speaking to the Indians in their own language, demonstrated how the needle always pointed to the north. The Indians decided to spare this fascinating man for a while. They took him to the village where Chief Powhatan (the tribe and their chief were both called Powhatan) was staying.

John Smith showing his compass to the Indians

Pomejack, Powhatan's village

After being led into Powhatan's lodge, Smith was questioned by the chief. Powhatan wanted to know why the Englishmen were in Virginia and when they would leave. Smith tried to lie his way out of trouble by saying that they had been driven there by a storm and would soon be leaving. Powhatan didn't believe him. Smith was sentenced to die for killing two Indians at the Chickahominy River battle.

Pocahontas rescues John Smith

Upon Powhatan's signal, two large stones were brought forth. The Indians grabbed John Smith, threw him to the ground, and forced his head onto the stones. When several braves raised their clubs above his head, Smith was certain that the end was near. But then the chief's daughter Pocahontas,* who was about twelve years old, ran

* For more information about Pocahontas see page 64

to Captain Smith and cradled his head in her arms. Several years later, Smith wrote the following description of this famous event:

> *Two great stones were brought before Powhatan; then as many as could laid hands on him [Smith], dragged him to them, and thereon laid his head, and being ready with their clubs, to beat out his brains, Pocahontas the King's dearest daughter, when no entreaty could prevail, got his head in her arms, and laid her own upon his to save him from death; whereat the Emperor was contented he should live.*

Although John Smith thought that Pocahontas had saved him on impulse, many historians think that the Indians did not really mean to kill Smith. They think that this dramatic event symbolized Pocahontas's "adoption" of the captain. Either way it is probable that Smith was saved because Pocahontas had taken a liking to him.

Smith exchanged pledges of friendship with Powhatan and then was escorted home. After this, Powhatan traded food to the colonists. He also taught them how to plant corn and make fishing traps. The settlers needed this help very much because, by the time Captain Smith returned to Jamestown in early January of 1608, only about

Statue of Pocahontas

forty of the original one hundred colonists were still living.

Soon after Captain Smith's return from Powhatan's village, Captain Christopher Newport arrived from England. He brought supplies and about 120 more colonists (including the first two women to arrive at Jamestown). The supplies helped the colony live through the rest of the winter. Unfortunately, few of the new men were the kind the colony needed. Like the original colonists, most of them did not know how to survive hardship or how to provide for themselves. When the London Company sent seventy more of this kind of men to Jamestown in September of 1608, Captain Smith was disgusted. He wrote the following letter to the colony's English sponsors:

> *When you send again I entreat you rather send but thirty carpenters, husbandmen, gardeners, fishermen, blacksmiths, masons, and diggers up of trees' roots, well-provided, than a thousand of such as we have. For except we be able to lodge and feed them, most will consume with want of necessaries before they can be made good for anything.*

Although deaths from disease continued throughout 1608, the hunger problem was not as bad as it had been earlier. Under the direction of Captain Smith, who was now the president of the colony, the colonists improved their settlement. The men cleared fields, built a blockhouse to strengthen their defense, and performed military drills.

A third shipment of much-needed supplies and additional colonists (which included women and children) arrived from England in September of 1609. Unfortunately, soon after this shipment, Captain Smith was badly wounded in a gunpowder explosion and had to return to England to regain his health.

When Smith left, there were almost five hundred colonists in the growing settlement of Jamestown. Although there were still occasional skirmishes with the Indians, Smith's friendship with Powhatan and Pocahontas had greatly improved the relations between the two groups. Things were looking good for the colony. But this situation did not last long.

Title page from a publication encouraging people to settle in Virginia, published by the London Company in 1609.

Guards, wearing the uniforms of the period, march through reconstructed Jamestown.

Chapter III

Years of Turmoil and Growth: 1609 to Mid-1700s

. . . the Church [was] down, the 16 palisades [were] broken, the bridge [was] in pieces, the well of fresh water [was] spoiled [because everyone] was dispersed all about, planting tobacco.

> *From a 1617 report explaining what happened when the Jamestown colonists discovered they could make money from tobacco*

The departure of John Smith in the fall of 1609 left the Jamestown Colony without a strong leader. The colonists still needed to get food from the Indians since they were not growing enough to feed themselves. Unfortunately, the colonists did not know how to deal with the Indians without the help of Smith, who had gained the respect and admiration of the Native Americans. When John Ratcliffe led thirty men out of Jamestown to bargain with the Powhatan Indians for food, the session ended in an argument and in the deaths of the Englishmen.

VIRGINIA
richly valued,

By the defcription of the maine land of Florida, her next neighbour:

Out of the foure yeeres continuall trauell and difcouerie, for aboue one thoufand miles Eaft and Weft, of *Don Ferdinando de Soto,* and fixe hundred able men in his companie.

Wherin are truly obferued the riches and fertilitie of thofe parts, abounding with things neceffarie, pleafant, and profitable for the life of man: with the natures and difpofitions of the Inhabitants.

Written by a Portugall gentleman of *Eluas,* emploied in all the action, and tranflated out of Portugefe by RICHARD HALLVYT.

AT LONDON

Printed by FELIX KYNGSTON for *Matthew Lownes,* and are to be fold at the figne of the Bifhops head in Pauls Churchyard.
1609.

The winter of 1609-10 was a time of such extreme famine in Jamestown that the few who survived later called it "the starving time." Day after day, more colonists died of hunger, disease, and cold. Instead of building badly needed new houses, the colonists tore down the old ones and burned them as firewood. Instead of trying to bargain with the Indians, the colonists helplessly watched as the Indians shot their arrows over the palisades surrounding the stricken town. When the colonists ran out of food, they ate their horses, then their dogs and cats, and finally rats, mice, snakes, and even dead human bodies.

By the spring of 1610, Jamestown had suffered a huge death toll. Out of about five hundred people who had lived in the town when John Smith left for England, only about sixty remained.

The survivors may have thought that they were seeing things when two small ships, carrying more than one hundred persons, arrived in Jamestown in May of 1610. These people had been sailing to Virginia a year earlier when their ship, the *Sea Venture*, was wrecked in Bermuda. The Jamestown colonists assumed they were dead. But the castaways had managed to survive in Bermuda and build two new ships out of the wreck of the *Sea Venture*. Among the persons aboard the two ships were a pipe-smoking young gentleman named John Rolfe who was to play a large part in the colony's development, and Sir Thomas Gates, who was sent over to be the acting governor of the colony.

The Jamestown colonists begged Gates to take them away in the two little ships. They wanted to go up to Newfoundland, in Canada. There they hoped to find some larger ships that could take them back to England. For two weeks Gates tried to talk them out of leaving the Jamestown Colony.

Finally, he took pity on the hungry and frightened colonists and agreed to take them away.

On a June day in 1610 the Jamestown survivors gathered up their few belongings and, to the beat of a drum, boarded the two small ships, the *Patience* and the *Deliverance*. The two ships sailed down the James and were approaching the open ocean when something remarkable happened. The departing colonists sighted a small boat approaching the Virginia shore. The men on the boat explained that three well-stocked English vessels were about to arrive. Hearing this, Sir Thomas Gates turned the *Patience* and the *Deliverance* around and returned to Jamestown. The Jamestown Colony had been saved, but it should be said that many of the survivors were disappointed. They would rather have gone back to England than return to the place where almost 90 percent of the colonists had died during the previous winter.

The fleet of three ships that reached Jamestown on June 10, 1610, was under the command of Thomas West, also called Lord De La Warr (1577-1618). Lord De La Warr, who had recently been named first governor of the Virginia Colony, brought much-needed food supplies with him. The ragged colonists lined up in military fashion to greet Lord De La Warr (for whom the colony and state of Delaware, Delaware Bay and River, and the Delaware Indians were later named). When the new English governor stepped ashore, followed by 150 new colonists, a sermon of thanksgiving was given.

Thomas West,
Lord De La Warr
(1577-1618)

Lord De La Warr governed the colonists with the same kind of discipline that John Smith had practiced. The fort and the houses were rebuilt, and the church was repaired. Lord De La Warr also had the streets and water well cleaned, which helped to make the colony more sanitary. By the time Lord De La Warr returned to England in March of 1611, the Virginia Colony was not only surviving—it was growing.

The colonists founded new towns. In 1610 colonists from Jamestown settled in Hampton, which is the oldest English-built town *still* standing in the United States today. In 1611 Henrico was founded, and more new towns were built soon after that. Building new towns in what the colonists called "the wilderness" meant that the Indians were slowly but surely losing more and more of their land.

Meanwhile, back in England, the investors in the Virginia Colony were unhappy. They had spent a fortune to support the colony but had received no gold or other riches in return. This changed in 1612 when John Rolfe* discovered that a valuable crop could be grown successfully in Virginia.

Rolfe, who was one of the Bermuda shipwreck survivors, ran out of pipe tobacco shortly after arriving in Virginia. The Indians gave Rolfe some of their tobacco, but he did not like the flavor. Rolfe then got several kinds of tobacco seed from a sea captain. Crossbreeding the different seeds (some of which had come from South America), Rolfe created a variety of tobacco that he found to be quite flavorful and mild. In 1613 Rolfe sent some of his tobacco to England, where experts declared that it was excellent. Suddenly there was a great demand in England for "Virginia tobacco."

The Virginia colonists gave up the search for gold and other riches. They cleared the woods, and planted millions of tobacco seeds. Tobacco was even grown in the middle of streets just to bring in a little more money. Thanks to John Rolfe, tobacco was on its way to becoming a big money-maker for Virginia and the London Company.

John Rolfe
(1585-1622)

* For more information about John Rolfe see page 65

44

Tobacco, not gold, brought wealth to the Virginia Colony.

Not only did John Rolfe help the Virginia Colony find a money-making crop, but he also helped to improve relations between the English and the Indians. He did it by falling in love.

In the spring of 1613, Samuel Argall, a sea captain who brought colonists to Jamestown and who often traded with the Indians for food, kidnapped Pocahontas and brought her to Jamestown. Later, Argall wrote that he wanted to ransom the Indian princess for "so many Englishmen as were prisoners with Powhatan" and to obtain "some quantity of corn for the

Romantic drawing of
the baptism of
Pocahontas

Colony's relief" from the chief. Pocahontas was taken to Henrico. She was treated with great respect, taught about Christianity, and christened with the new name Rebecca.

In the summer of 1613, Pocahontas met John Rolfe, and the two soon fell in love. When Pocahontas sent her father a message about her proposed marriage to Rolfe, the old chief was pleased. He made a peace pledge to the colonists and sent several relatives to the wedding, which was held in April of 1614.

Largely because of this marriage, there was little fighting between the Indians and the Virginia colonists for the next eight years. The colony grew rapidly. Each year hundreds of new colonists arrived, more land was cleared, and more tobacco was sold in England. By 1619 the population of Virginia was almost twenty-two hundred, and the colony was exporting more than twenty tons of tobacco each year.

Pocahontas
(c. 1595-1617)

Starting with Lord De La Warr, the Virginia Colony had been ruled only by a governor who was appointed by the London Company. Some of the governors were tyrants in the eyes of the Virginia colonists. For example, Sir Thomas Dale, who was

Sir Thomas Dale became governor in 1611. He found the colonists lazy and he forced them to work or go to jail. Some colonists called the years of his reign—1611 to 1616—"five years of slavery."

called the "Iron Governor," severely punished colonists who broke his strict laws. As the Virginia Colony became more successful, the colonists wanted to have a part in governing themselves.

In 1619 the London Company allowed the Virginia colonists a certain amount of self-government. The settled part of Virginia was divided up into eleven sections called boroughs. In an election that was open to all free adult males, each borough elected two men called burgesses to a lawmaking body called the House of Burgesses, which met in Jamestown. The

House of Burgesses met for the first time on July 30, 1619. In its first session it passed laws governing relations with the Indians. It also set prices for tobacco and outlawed drunkenness and gambling.

Shipload of brides
arrives at Jamestown.

House of Burgesses, whose decisions could be
overruled by the governor, met for the first time
on July 30, 1619. This was the first lawmaking
body in what is now the United States that was
made up of elected representatives. Virginia's
state legislature of today is an outgrowth of the
House of Burgesses.

The year that the House of Burgesses was
founded, two groups of people arrived who were to
play important roles in the future of the Virginia
Colony. One was a group of nearly one hundred
young ladies who sailed in the first "bride-ship"
to reach Virginia. These young ladies, who were

TO BE SOLD, on board the
Ship *Bance-Iſland*, on tueſday the 6th
of *May* next, at *Aſhley-Ferry*; a choice
cargo of about 250 fine healthy
NEGROES,
juſt arrived from the
Windward & Rice Coaſt.
—The utmoſt care has
already been taken, and
ſhall be continued, to keep them free from
the leaſt danger of being infected with the
SMALL-POX, no boat having been on
board, and all other communication with
people from *Charles-Town* prevented.
Auſtin, Laurens, & Appleby.

N. B. Full one Half of the above Negroes have had the
SMALL-POX in their own Country.

Poster advertising
slaves for sale

interested in marriage, were sent over at the London Company's expense. A colonist who married one of them had to pay the London Company 120 pounds of tobacco for her passage to Virginia. Within several years nearly all the young women had married Virginia tobacco planters and had children. Virginia's population grew.

The second group to arrive in Virginia in 1619 had been taken there against their will. On a summer day in 1619, a Dutch trading ship, carrying about twenty black slaves, arrived at Jamestown, where the slaves were "sold" for supplies. At this time many of Virginia's white colonists were "indentured servants"—people who agreed to work for a certain time, usually for seven years, for planters who paid for their passage to the New World. At first the blacks in Virginia were treated more like indentured servants than slaves. Blacks could earn their freedom after working for their masters for several years. However, by the late 1600s most of the blacks in Virginia were slaves. They were forced to work for their masters and could not earn their freedom.

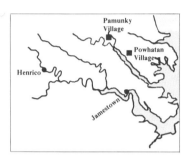

Meanwhile, the Indians were about to revolt. When Pocahontas died of smallpox in 1617 while on a visit to England with her husband, John Rolfe, the colonists lost one of their best Indian friends. The next year Powhatan, the greatest peacekeeper among the Indians, died. The new chief was Opechancanough, Powhatan's half brother, who had captured John Smith on the Chickahominy River ten years earlier. Opechancanough hated the English for having stolen Indian land. He planned to destroy them in a surprise attack on March 22, 1622.

Because they were getting along well with the Indians, the colonists were not prepared for the attack. In fact, many of them invited the Indians

De Bry engraving
showing massacre
of 1622

Chanco takes the warning to Jamestown.

into their homes to eat breakfast or to trade as usual on that Good Friday morning. Suddenly, in eighty different places in Virginia, the Indians turned on the colonists with tomahawks, knives, and arrows.

By the time the attack was over about 350 of Virginia's 2,200 colonists were dead. The toll would have been far worse, but an Indian boy named Chanco had warned the Jamestown colonists the night before. Thanks to him the people in Virginia's capital were able to defend themselves.

This massacre led to a major political change in Virginia. England's King James I decided that the London Company had handled Indian relations and several other matters poorly. In May of 1624 he took the colony away from the London Company. Virginia became a royal colony. Now it

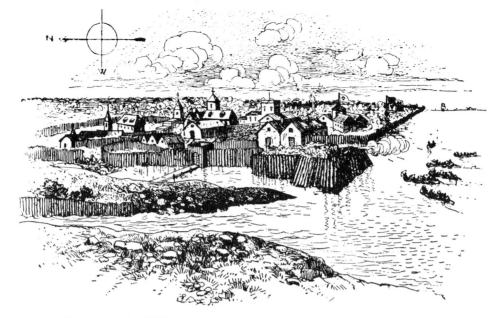

Jamestown in 1622

was under the direct control of the king, who sent royal governors to rule for him. England was having problems of its own, however, and for much of the time between 1624 and 1660 the mother country allowed the Virginia colonists almost complete control of their affairs. Those royal governors who did try to make the colony obey them were usually disliked by the Virginians, who were becoming used to ruling themselves.

Meanwhile, the colonists were getting revenge for the Good Friday massacre by burning Indian villages and killing hundreds of Indians, including many who had not taken part in the massacre. In turn, the Indians planned new attacks, including some that killed about five hundred colonists in April of 1644. The colonists had better weapons, however, and these helped them defeat the Indians and push them farther and farther west.

The flight of the Indians opened up more Virginia land for colonization. According to a 1637 law, anyone who settled on unoccupied Virginia land and built a house on it received a grant of fifty acres of land. This was an attractive offer to land-hungry persons in the crowded country of England. By 1650 the Virginia Colony was home to about twenty thousand non-Indians, including fifteen thousand free whites, five thousand indentured whites, and three hundred black servants and slaves.

Colonists planted tobacco for money and corn for food.

By this time, tobacco was the leading farm crop in Virginia, which was nicknamed "the tobacconized colony." Tobacco was the main source of income for both wealthy plantation owners and smaller farmers. The "green gold" was even used as money for paying salaries, taxes, fines, and debts. Because their incomes depended on how much money their tobacco earned in England, the price of tobacco was important. Many Virginia planters were becoming more and more angry about the low prices that England was paying them for their tobacco. In time, their anger helped bring about a revolt against Virginia's English rulers.

In 1660 Charles II took the throne in England and soon made trouble in faraway Virginia. For one thing, Charles II gave some Virginia land to his noblemen friends. This angered the colonists. The Virginians were also angry about taxes put on their tobacco exports. They objected to the new laws that stopped them from trading with countries outside the British Empire that might give them better prices for their tobacco. Also, in 1660 Charles II made the poor choice of Sir

King Charles II (1630-1685). Called the Merry Monarch, Charles ruled from 1660 to 1685, but he was not liked. The Earl of Rochester said of him: "Here lies our sovereign lord, the king, whose word no man relies on; who never said a foolish thing, and never did a wise one."

Tobacco ships on the
James River

William Berkeley (1606-77) as royal governor of
Virginia.

Berkeley had been governor of Virginia from
1642 to 1652 and had been popular during that
first term. However, during his second term he
upset the colonists by limiting their political
power and refusing to help defend them against
Indian attacks in the mid-1670s.

In 1676 some Virginia landowners chose
Nathaniel Bacon (1647-76) to lead them against
the Indians. Bacon, who owned a tobacco
plantation within the borders of present-day
Richmond, Virginia, led an army that killed a

Bacon confronts
Governor Berkeley.

large number of Indians, including some who had
been friendly with the colonists. Hatred of the
Indians was so strong at the time that most of the
colonists approved of these murders.

After defeating the Indians, Bacon asked
Governor Berkeley to make several governmental
reforms. The seventy-year-old Berkeley angrily
refused and called Bacon "the greatest rebel that
ever was in Virginia!" Berkeley even walked out of
the statehouse in Jamestown and challenged the
younger man to fight him in a duel. In the

summer of 1676 Bacon and his followers surrounded the statehouse, forced Governor Berkeley to flee, then burned Jamestown. Bacon's Rebellion, as it was called, collapsed when Nathaniel Bacon became ill and died in October of 1676. After that, the leaders of the rebellion were arrested, and more than twenty of them were executed by the government.

An important event, a more peaceful one, happened in 1693. The College of William and Mary (named after William III and Mary II, England's reigning king and queen) was founded at a town called the Middle Plantation, seven miles from Jamestown. This was the Virginia

STRANGE NEWS
FROM
VIRGINIA:
Being a full and true
ACCOUNT
OF THE
LIFE and DEATH
OF
Nathanael Bacon Esquire,
Who was the only Cause and Original of all the late Troubles in that COUNTRY.
With a full Relation of all the Accidents which have happened in the late War there between the Christians and Indians.

LONDON,
Printed for William Harris, next door to the Turn-Stile without Moor-gate. 1677.

Handbill, printed in London in 1677, gives the government's account of Bacon's Rebellion.

Bacon's army burns Jamestown.

College of William and Mary

William III of Orange
(1650-1702) was king
of England (1689-
1702). Mary II, (1662-
1694) was his wife.

Colony's first college, and today it is second only to Harvard University (which was founded in 1636) as the oldest institution of higher education in the United States. In 1699 the name of the Middle Plantation was changed to Williamsburg, in honor of William III. That same year, Williamsburg became the capital of Virginia, replacing Jamestown, which had suffered a disastrous fire in 1698.

According to its charter, the colony occupied more land than what is now the state of Virginia.

Williamsburg is a restored colonial village.

In fact, because all or part of nine states (Illinois, Indiana, Kentucky, Michigan, Minnesota, Ohio, Virginia, West Virginia, and Wisconsin) were once part of the colony. Virginia is sometimes called the Mother of States. By 1700 the population of the Virginia Colony was about 62,800. Almost all the people lived in the Tidewater, the name for the one-hundred-mile-wide strip of land along the Atlantic Ocean.

Many of the Tidewater planters owned huge, sprawling farms called plantations, which did not leave much room for newcomers in the region. Because of this, many people wanted to move to the western part of what is now the state of

Shirley Plantation

Virginia. First, however, they needed to learn more
about the land.

In 1710 Alexander Spotswood (1676-1740) was
named acting governor of Virginia. Spotswood
recognized that the Virginians badly wanted to
move westward, so, in 1716, he organized an
expedition. Spotswood himself led the expedition
and took with him more than sixty men on
horseback. The Spotswood expedition headed
west beyond the Piedmont and over the Blue
Ridge Mountains, stopping along the way to hunt

Virginia forest

Alexander Spotswood explored the land west of the Blue Ridge Mountains.

deer and bear in Virginia's beautiful forests and to fish in its sky-blue rivers. Finally, the men entered a breathtaking, beautiful valley that the Indians called Shanando, meaning Daughter of the Stars. Changing the name slightly, the explorers named the valley and the river that flows through it Shenandoah.

Upon their return to Williamsburg, Spotswood and the others raved about the rivers, valleys, mountains, and forests that they saw on their expedition. The stories of these and other explorers lured more people to the colony. As a result, by 1730 Virginia's population grew to 114,000. By 1740 it was almost 180,000, with many of the newcomers working small farms in the valleys of what are now central and western Virginia.

POCAHONTAS (About 1595-1617)

Exactly when and where the Indian girl named Matoaka was born is not known, but it probably was in eastern Virginia around 1595. When the Jamestown colonists arrived in 1607, Matoaka was about twelve years old. Little is known about Matoaka's life away from the colonists, but when she was with them, she lived up to her Indian nickname, Pocahontas, which means "The Playful One."

After Pocahontas saved John Smith's life in early 1608, there was a short time of peace between the colonists and the Indians. During this time Pocahontas often came to Jamestown, where she would challenge the young men to compete with her at performing handsprings and running races. The English youths taught her a phrase: "Love you not me?" which Pocahontas would repeat to them. In return, Pocahontas taught Captain Smith and the other colonists some Indian words.

In the spring of 1608, John Smith got into an argument with Pocahontas's people during a bargaining session and took seven of them captive. Powhatan tried to get the prisoners released, but nothing worked until he sent Pocahontas to Jamestown as his agent. Captain Smith and the other leaders of Jamestown let the prisoners go for the sake of the Indian girl.

About a year after this incident, Smith left Virginia, and relations between the Indians and the colonists worsened. Those few times when the Indians and the colonists met peacefully, Pocahontas and her people asked what had become of Captain Smith. The colonists always said that he was dead.

In 1613 Pocahontas was staying in an Indian village along the Potomac River when she was kidnapped and taken first to Jamestown and then to Henrico. In Henrico she was given fancy English petticoats and dresses to replace her deerskin clothes, taught the English language, and renamed Rebecca. How Pocahontas felt about this brainwashing program we do not know. We do know, however, that Pocahontas met the tobacco planter John Rolfe in the summer of 1613 and that the next spring the two were married in a ceremony that was Jamestown's big social event of the year.

In 1616 Pocahontas and her husband went with their year-old son, Thomas, and several other Indians to England. She was introduced to royalty and invited to balls and banquets. In England, Pocahontas also learned a startling piece of news: John Smith was still alive! One day in the fall of 1616 Captain Smith called at the house where she was staying near London.

Pocahontas, who by this time was ill because of England's damp and chilly weather, was both pleased and upset at the sight of Smith. "They did tell us always you were dead," she said. Pocahontas then teased Smith for having forgotten her, reminded him that she had adopted him long ago, and called him "Father." When Smith said that she should not call him "Father," Pocahontas answered, "I tell you then I will, and I will be forever and ever your countryman."

A few minutes later Captain Smith left, and the two never met again. In March of 1617, just as the Rolfes were about to sail home to Virginia, Pocahontas died of smallpox. The woman who had saved John Smith's life and who had once performed handsprings in Jamestown was only twenty-two years old when she died. Thomas Rolfe, her son, was educated in England. At age twenty he returned to Virginia, where he became a popular citizen and even helped defend the colony against the Indians.

JOHN ROLFE (1585-1622)

Born in the village of Heachem, England, John Rolfe decided to seek his fortune in the New World shortly after he was married around 1608. In the summer of 1609 Rolfe and his wife (whose first name is unknown) sailed for Virginia with Captain Christopher Newport and about 150 others in the *Sea Venture*. The ship sailed into a hurricane and was wrecked on the island of Bermuda, about seven hundred miles from Jamestown.

While on the island, Mrs. Rolfe gave birth to a daughter, who was named Bermuda, but the little girl soon died. The castaways managed to build two little ships and then sailed into Jamestown in May of 1610. Soon after their arrival, Mrs. Rolfe died.

Rolfe, who grew tobacco in Virginia for his own use, began the colony's tobacco industry. "Virginia tobacco," which helped to save the colony and bring it prosperity, is still the state's leading farm crop.

In 1613 Rolfe met Pocahontas (probably in church) and soon was helping the Indian princess with her English lessons and reading to her from the Bible. Rolfe realized that a marriage between himself and Pocahontas would help the colony, but he also believed that "My heartie and best thoughts are . . . intangled and inthralled," which was a seventeenth-century way of saying that he was in love!

After Pocahontas's death in England in early 1617, Rolfe returned to Virginia, where he married for a third time and served on the governing council. Some say that Rolfe died in the big Indian attack of March 22, 1622, while others think that he already had been dead for several days when this massacre occurred.

Mount Vernon, like other plantations in Virginia, was built on the edge of a river.

Chapter IV

Life in Colonial Virginia

They live in so happy a climate and have so fertile a soil that nobody [among the white Virginians] is poor.

Slaves are the Negroes and their posterity. . . . They are called slaves in respect of the time of their servitude because it is for life.

The Indians of Virginia are almost wasted—all which together can't raise five hundred fighting men. They live poorly and much in fear.

> Robert Beverley, The History and Present State of Virginia (1705)

Colonial seal of Virginia

Colonial Virginia was home to people of vastly different life-styles. While the plantation owners were living in luxury, their black field hands were living in poverty. While the less wealthy white farmers were carving homesteads out of the wilderness, the Indians were being forced to retreat from their Virginia homelands. What follows is a description of how these four groups of Virginians lived around the year 1740.

Artist's drawing of a wealthy plantation family surrounded by slaves.
Drawn a hundred years ago, this picture represents the slaves
negatively. They appear to be courting favor by bowing to their owners.

WEALTHY PLANTATION OWNERS

Although there were never more than several
hundred extremely wealthy plantation owners in
colonial Virginia, these were the people who held
the most power. Often the wealthiest Virginians,
who lived mainly in the Tidewater region, owned
several plantations. One, Robert Carter, owned a
total of forty-two plantations!

Tobacco was king on the plantations, which were usually built near rivers. Ships would sail up the rivers and then anchor at the plantations' private docks. The tobacco would be loaded onto the ships, which would then transport it to England. There, merchants would sell the tobacco, keep their own earnings, then deposit the remaining money in the planters' bank accounts. The money they made from the tobacco allowed the wealthy planters to build grand homes.

Leading to a typical plantation house was a magnificent avenue bordered by such trees as tulips, cedars, or oaks. Beautiful gardens and reflecting pools surrounded the house. Many of the plantation houses were architectural masterpieces with beautiful white columns, winding staircases, and a dozen or more rooms with high ceilings.

Canoes, boats, wagons, and rolling barrels were used to transport tobacco to the ships that would take it to England.

Plantation owners imported many items from England, not only because the mother country was superior to Virginia in manufacturing, but also because they liked to copy the life-style of the wealthy English aristocrats. The wooden furniture in the plantation houses usually came from England, as did most of the silver, china,

Parties were a basic part of plantation life.

A collection of silver, identified as the Brandon plate

paintings, books, and silk and velvet clothes.

Servants, dressed in fancy uniforms, took care of all the needs of the plantation family. They served the family their meals in the dining room, brought them their tea in the parlor, dressed them when it was time to go out, and drove the family around the countryside in their four-horse carriage.

The fortunes earned from tobacco gave the wealthy plantation families plenty of time for recreation. Balls and concerts were held regularly at various plantations, and these would attract

Hunting was a favorite sport.

people for miles around. Card playing, hunting, horse racing, and cockfighting were other popular pastimes among the wealthy aristocrats. Perhaps most popular of all was "visiting." One family would visit with another for several weeks and then play host to that family for several weeks after that.

For many of the planters, the two Publick Times held in Williamsburg were the two highlights of the year. At the Publick Times, planters would attend meetings of Virginia's highest court, which was called the General Court. The planters would also do business with one another and attend balls, fairs, plays, and horse races while in the capital city.

The children of the plantation owners were pampered and fussed over like princes and princesses. The girls were given miniature tea

Elegant hall in Carter's Grove, an old colonial mansion on the James River

Many plantation owners felt the best that money could buy came only from England. Here we see seventeenth-century parents watching their children perform a dance of the period, the minuet.

sets and dolls in silk dresses. The boys played with miniature armies, tops, and marbles. In many households servants took care of all the children's needs, dressing them in the morning, cutting up their meat for them at mealtime, and singing them to sleep at night.

The children of the wealthy planters usually were educated by tutors who came to their homes. When they were old enough to go to college, some of the young men went to England to complete their education. Others went to the new College of William and Mary in Williamsburg.

Engraving shows slaves working in the tobacco fields.

BLACK SLAVES

As the white plantation owners sat drinking brandy or tea in their roomy parlors, their black slaves were living in cramped cabins not far from the plantation houses. Mainly because the plantation owners wanted help with their tobacco crop, the slave population grew quickly during

Young mistress of the plantation brings Christmas gifts to a slave family.

the early 1700s. In 1700 there were about 6,000 black slaves in Virginia out of a population of about 62,800. By 1730 more than one fourth of the colony's 114,000 people were black slaves, and by 1740 there were more blacks than there were whites in Virginia.

Although some plantation owners were kind to their slaves and although some house slaves lived rather nicely, the life of a slave was mostly one of extreme hardship. After awakening at daybreak, the field slaves dressed in their coarse cotton clothes, ate a breakfast of corn cakes, and then went out to work. They worked in the fields all day with only one or two breaks. When the sun set on the tobacco fields, the slaves were sent to the tobacco houses, where they worked for several hours preparing the harvested tobacco. The exhausted slaves finally were led back to their cabins, where they slept for a few hours on their homemade bunks before awakening for a new day's work.

Plantation team

From time to time, slaves who were treated this way ran away from their masters. They had no chance to escape across the Atlantic Ocean to their African homelands and little chance of hiding from their masters for very long. A slave usually would be lashed brutally for running away, and a slave who was accused of lying might have an ear nailed to a post for an hour, after which the ear would be cut off. Slaves who stole from their masters were sometimes killed. It should be added that most masters did not treat their slaves too brutally because slaves were considered valuable property.

Very few slaves were taught to read and write. The plantation owners were afraid that if the slaves were able to read and write they might plan a large-scale rebellion. Even though the slaves had many hardships and rules they had to obey, they still found ways to enjoy themselves after their workweek ended on Saturday afternoon. On Saturday night they would get together to dance and to sing songs that many years later would influence jazz music. On Sundays the slaves who had been baptized would go to church. Sunday was also the day when the slaves would work in their little family gardens and rest up for the long workweek ahead.

FARM FAMILIES

Among Virginia's white population, the wealthy plantation owners were a minority. Most of the

Virginia
mountaineer
with his son

Settler's home in the wilderness

white colonists were farmers who had to work almost all the time just to feed their families. By 1740 these hardworking farm families moved to what is now central and western Virginia. Among the colonists who settled in these areas were people of English and also German, Swiss, and Scotch-Irish background. Towns grew up in places where several dozen families settled near each other.

The families who settled in "the wilderness" chopped down trees and built log cabins. They also built their tables, beds, and other furniture

A Currier and Ives
lithograph showing
hunters bringing
food home

out of wood. The cracks between the logs in their
cabins often were not chinked very well with clay
or moss, so people were able to see the stars
shining through their ceilings as they lay in bed
at night!

Fireplaces kept the log cabins warm at night
and during the wintertime. Food was also cooked
over the fireplaces in big pots. The frontier
families had to find all their own food. Both men
and women hunted deer, bear, and other wild
game. The settlers ate the meat and, like the
Indians, made clothes out of the animal skins.
One of the favorite foods on the frontier was corn,
which many people ate in different forms for

breakfast, lunch, and dinner. Other favorites were soups and stews, including vegetable-and-squirrel stew.

The frontier children spent most of their time helping their parents farm, hunt, and make clothes and furniture. The wealthy planters who controlled Virginia's political life were not interested in free public schools for the people. Because of this, the children of the farm families usually grew up with little or no education. Parents who could read, write, and "cipher" taught these subjects to their children, but these skills were not thought to be as important on the frontier as knowing how to plant corn or shoot a gun. The children were often taught to shoot as soon as they could hold and aim a rifle. Shooting

Woodcut showing an early method of pounding corn

Colonial pantry was called a larder.

Sassafras was used to make tea.

was important not only for bringing home food but also for protection against the Indians.

In many areas of the frontier, there were no doctors within a hundred miles or more. When members of the family got sick, frontier mothers tried to make them better with home cures. Sassafras tea was supposed to be good for curing fevers and headaches. Tobacco was supposed to be good for curing snakebites, stomachaches, toothaches, and even bad breath!

Because the families felt isolated and alone on the frontier, they especially enjoyed the times when they could get together with their neighbors. Because husking corn was boring, the people held "cornhusking bees." When a new family moved into an area, their neighbors got together with them for a "house-raising." While the men and older boys put the finishing touches on the new family's house, the women had quilting bees, and the children played such games as fox-in-the-warren, leapfrog, and tag. Once the new family's house was finished, the people would hold a party. They would barbecue food, play the fiddle, dance, and drink homemade corn whiskey and apple cider.

Colonial shopkeeper and customer

THE INDIANS

There were never very many Indians in Virginia. It is estimated that when the first English colonists arrived in 1607, there were fewer than twenty thousand Indians there. A hundred years later, Virginia was home to only several thousand Indians.

The population of the Native Americans got smaller for several reasons. Many died of smallpox and other diseases that were brought to Virginia by the Europeans. Some of the Indians were killed in battle by the better weapons of the newcomers. Many others were forced to leave after their chiefs were tricked into signing treaties that gave up their land.

During the early 1700s, most of the Indians that were still in Virginia lived in the western part of the colony. A treaty signed in 1722 said that the Indians needed a written pass just to cross Virginia's Blue Ridge Mountains into eastern Virginia. The Indians did not want to go near the colonists' towns and plantations anyway because they were afraid of being shot by Indian-hating whites. Settlers who shot Indians were rarely brought to justice because most of the colonists "scarcely consider (the Indians) as of the human species," as one English traveler in Virginia wrote in the 1750s.

To support their part of the 1722 treaty, the colonists were supposed to stay out of Indian lands west of the Blue Ridge Mountains. However, the colonists did not obey this part of the agreement. More and more white settlers moved west, pushing more and more Indians out of western Virginia. By the eve of the revolutionary war, the few remaining Indians in Virginia were strangers in a land that once had been all theirs.

Pushed off their land the Indians retreated west into the forests.

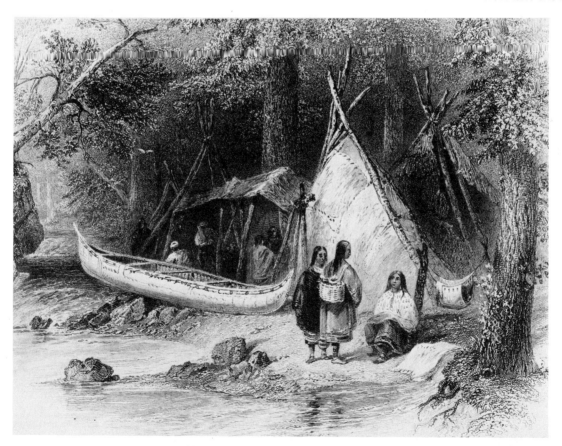

Many Indian tribes fought with the French against the British.

Chapter V

The Revolutionary War Begins

Is life so dear, or peace so sweet, as to be purchased at the price of chains and slavery? Forbid it, Almighty God! I know not what course others may take, but as for me, give me liberty or give me death!

Patrick Henry, in a speech to the Second Virginia Convention, March 23, 1775

By the middle of the 1700s Great Britain was quarreling with both the French and the Indians over land in America. The conflict with the French was over a huge region that stretched from the Mississippi River to the Appalachian Mountains. The Indians were angry at the British for having steadily pushed them off their ancestral lands.

The Indians and the French got along rather well with each other, mainly because the French were more interested in trading for furs than in seizing Indian land. In fact, the French and the

HUDSON BAY
COMPANY

CANADA
(to England)

Miquelon &
St. Pierre
(French)

(to England)

THIRTEEN ENGLISH COLONIES

Proclamation Line of 1763

LOUISIANA
(to Spain)

North America
after the treaty
of
1763

FLORIDA
(to England)

George Washington leads a retreat.

Indians often lived close to each other. Many French fur traders were married to Indian women. The British had Indian friends, too, but they were fewer in number than those who sided with the French.

From 1754 to 1763 the French and their Indian allies fought a war against the British and their Indian allies. This war is known as the French and Indian War. Little of the fighting took place in what is now Virginia. But as one of the most populous and richest of Great Britain's thirteen American colonies, Virginia played a major role in providing men and supplies for the war effort.

One Virginian who distinguished himself during this war was a young man named George Washington. In the early years of the fighting, Washington carried messages through enemy territory, captured French prisoners, and directed the building of Fort Necessity (located near present-day Pittsburgh, Pennsylvania). He risked death many times while leading Virginia soldiers against the French and the Indians. In those first years of the war it appeared that the British might lose. Later, however, their superior numbers of troops and weapons enabled the British to win.

To protest the Stamp Act, the *Pennsylvania Journal & Advertiser* sarcastically suggested this skull and crossbone stamp be put on all goods imported from Great Britain.

Although victorious, Britain faced several financial problems. Who would pay the debt the country had incurred while fighting the war? Who would pay to keep the army and navy needed to protect Britain's newly won lands? British lawmakers decided that the American colonies should pay some of these costs. After all, pointed out British lawmakers, the war had been fought in part to protect the American colonists against the French and the Indians.

During the 1760s Great Britain placed a number of taxes on the American colonies. The Stamp Act of 1765 required Americans to buy

Colonists throw Stamp Act papers into a bonfire.

stamps and place them on all official documents and newspapers. Taxes were also put on paper, molasses, tea, and other items that were imported into the colonies.

These taxes angered the American colonists. They gathered in taverns and meeting halls from New York to Georgia to discuss the problem. "Taxation without representation is tyranny!" became their cry. This meant that they resented having to pay high taxes to the mother country while having no say in the British lawmaking body called the Parliament.

Laws banned Americans from buying many items from non-British nations. But to avoid paying the taxes on imported British products, Americans smuggled goods from other nations into Boston and other seaports. Many Americans also boycotted (refused to buy) anything shipped from England. For example, instead of drinking tea shipped by British companies, the colonists made tea using currant leaves, sassafras, and other plants.

Taxation wasn't the sole reason that Americans were discontented with British rule. By the 1760s many of the colonial families had lived in America

American patriots published the names of those people who refused to stop buying and selling British goods.

Tax collector hanged
in effigy by patriots

for several generations. These people tended to think of themselves as Americans, not English. They resented being ruled by a nation three thousand miles away that most of them had never even seen.

During the 1760s a few colonists began to speak of freeing the American colonies from Great Britain—even if a war was required. The British considered such talk treasonous. That didn't stop several brave souls, including Samuel Adams of Massachusetts and Patrick Henry of Virginia, from speaking out.

Patrick Henry* was a lawyer and member of the House of Burgesses from Louisa County, which was then considered the Virginia backwoods. On May 29, 1765, Patrick Henry introduced seven resolutions into the House of Burgesses condemning Great Britain for imposing the Stamp Act on the colonies. Three of Henry's resolutions read:

1. Resolved, That the first adventurers and settlers of this, his majesty's colony and dominion, brought with them and transmitted to their posterity . . . all the privileges, franchises, and immunities that have at any time been held, enjoyed, and possessed, by the people of Great Britain.
3. Resolved, That the taxation of the people by themselves or by persons chosen by themselves to

* For more information about Patrick Henry see page 135

represent them ... is the distinguishing characteristic of British freedom. ...

6. Resolved, That his majesty's liege people, the inhabitants of this colony, are not bound to yield obedience to any law or ordinance whatever, designed to impose any taxation whatsoever upon them, other than the laws or ordinances of the General Assembly [House of Burgesses] aforesaid.

George III
(1738-1820)

According to a young Virginian named Thomas Jefferson, who attended the House of Burgesses meeting on that spring day in 1765, Patrick Henry's resolutions inspired a "most bloody" debate. Most of the other burgesses were wealthy men who did business with England and were reluctant to criticize the mother country. To these men, Henry's suggestion that Americans "are not bound to yield obedience" to unjust laws was treasonous.

While defending his proposals, Patrick Henry went into a now famous tirade about the king of Great Britain, George III. "Caesar had his Brutus!" he cried. "Charles the First his Cromwell! And George the Third—"

Brutus had led the plot to kill Caesar, and Cromwell had signed Charles I's death warrant. Fearing that Patrick Henry was about to suggest the murder of the king, the burgesses screamed, "Treason! Treason!"

Patrick Henry
(1736-1799)

"—And George the Third may profit by their example," continued the great speaker, who concluded by saying, "If this be treason, make the most of it!"

Three of Patrick Henry's proposals (including #6) were too radical for the burgesses. But when the debate ended, they passed the other four. These resolutions, called the Virginia Resolves, were published in newspapers throughout the colonies and helped inspire the rising tide of anger towards Britain. Years later, when reviewing Patrick Henry's contribution to the American cause, Thomas Jefferson said that the great speaker had started "the ball of revolution" rolling.

Patrick Henry had a reputation as a wild radical. During the next few years some very steady and cautious Americans began to talk of revolution. One such person was George Washington.* From his plantation Mount Vernon near Alexandria, Virginia, Washington wrote this letter to his friend and neighbor George Mason:

JOIN or DIE

Patriots wanted all the colonies to work together for liberty.

Mount Vernon, April 5, 1769
. . . . At a time when our lordly Masters in Great Britain will be satisfied with nothing less than the

---

* For more information about George Washington see page 134

South front of Mount Vernon, Washington's plantation home

deprication of American freedom, it seems highly necessary that some thing shou'd be done to avert the stroke and maintain the liberty which we have derived from our Ancestors; but the manner of doing it to answer the purpose effectually is the point in question.

That no man shou'd scruple, or hesitate a moment to use a-ms in defence of so valuable a blessing, on which all the good and evil of life depends; is clearly my opinion; yet A-ms I wou'd beg leave to add, should be the last resource. . . .

By "a-ms" George Washington meant arms, or weapons. In case you are wondering why he left out the *r*, imagine someone today writing a letter about the possible overthrow of the government. He or she would be in big trouble if this letter were seen by government officials. Likewise, Washington would have had problems if the British got hold of his letter. By writing "a-ms" he could claim, if need be, that he had really meant "alms."

On the Death of Five young Men who was Murthered, *March* 5th 1770. By the 29th Regiment.

The five men killed in the Boston Massacre were remembered by this notice.

Like George Washington, most Americans thought that arms should only be used as a "last resource." But as time passed it appeared that arms were the colonists' *only* resource. Again and again King George III and the British Parliament ignored American complaints. George III felt that the Americans were disloyal to the mother country and should be disciplined like naughty children. Although by 1770 Parliament had removed most of the taxes it had placed on the colonies, the hated tea tax was kept just so that the Americans would know who was in charge.

The hotbed of American unrest during these years was Boston, Massachusetts. More than the people of any other city, Bostonians defied British tax collectors and held meetings to protest British injustice. The Bostonians were so rebellious that in 1768 Britain had sent in troops to try to keep order in the city.

The Bostonians pelted the British soldiers with snowballs and called them "lobsterbacks" (because of their red uniforms). Generally the soldiers ignored these taunts. But on March 5, 1770, British soldiers suddenly fired into an angry crowd of Bostonians, killing five of them.

94

Engraving by Paul Revere entitled "The Bloody Massacre perpetrated in King Street, Boston on March 5, 1770 by a part of the 29th Regiment"

Although this incident was really more like a street brawl, Sam Adams and others called it a "massacre." The "Boston Massacre" was the most famous of the skirmishes fought between the British and the American colonists before the outbreak of actual war.

On December 16, 1773, Boston was the site of another famous prewar event. Dressed as Indians, fifty colonists boarded three British ships and dumped 340 chests of tea into Boston

Map of the
thirteen colonies

Dramatic painting recalls the Boston Tea Party

Harbor. This "Boston Tea Party" was staged to protest the tax on tea. To punish Bostonians for this act, Great Britain ordered the port of Boston closed until the destroyed tea was paid for. Although the port closing meant food shortages and other hardships for them, Bostonians decided at a town meeting that they wouldn't pay for the tea.

News of the closing of Boston's port spread throughout the colonies. In Williamsburg, Virginia, more than five hundred miles from Boston, some of the colonial leaders decided that they should show support for the Massachusetts patriots. Thomas Jefferson, Patrick Henry, Richard Henry Lee, Francis Lightfoot Lee, and several others formed a plan. The burgesses would spend the day that the port of Boston was first closed—June 1, 1774—in prayer and fasting.

John Murray, Earl of Dunmore (1732-1809)

This proposed gesture of unity with the Boston patriots angered the British governor of Virginia, John Murray, the Earl of Dunmore. Late in May, Lord Dunmore told the burgesses that their actions made "it necessary for me to dissolve you, and you are dissolved accordingly."

After the closing of the House, the burgesses marched up Williamsburg's Duke of Gloucester Street to the Raleigh Tavern. There they declared "that an attack made on one of our sister colonies is an attack made on all British America and threatens ruin to the rights of all." They also decided a meeting of representatives from all the colonies was needed to discuss American grievances against Great Britain.

Patrick Henry addresses the First Virginia Convention.

In summer of 1774, plans for a general meeting were made. Each colony was to choose several representatives to attend the meeting, which was to be held in Philadelphia, Pennsylvania. In August of 1774 the Virginia burgesses met again at the Raleigh Tavern at what was called the First Virginia Convention. At this meeting they chose seven delegates to attend the general congress. The seven Virginians chosen were Richard Bland,

Benjamin Harrison (the father of President William Henry Harrison and great-grandfather of President Benjamin Harrison), Patrick Henry, Richard Henry Lee, Edmund Pendleton, Peyton Randolph, and George Washington.

The First Continental Congress opened in Philadelphia on September 5, 1774. Fifty-six delegates representing twelve colonies (Georgia had sent no delegates) attended. Peyton Randolph, a planter and lawyer from Williamsburg, Virginia, was chosen president of the Congress. The fiery Patrick Henry set the mood of unity when he told the delegates on the second day of the Congress:

Richard Henry Lee
(c. 1732-1794)

> *The distinctions between Virginians,*
> *Pennsylvanians, New Yorkers, and New Englanders*
> *are no more. I am not a Virginian, but an American!*

The purpose of the First Continental Congress was to denounce British taxes and other injustices. Most of the delegates wanted America to obtain better treatment from the mother country while remaining part of the British Empire. However, Patrick Henry and some of the other radical delegates wanted to form a separate country. Plans were even discussed for arming the

Peyton Randolph
(c. 1721-1775)

Carpenters' Hall,
Philadelphia

colonists in case of war with Great Britain.

After the First Continental Congress adjourned in late October of 1774, the delegates returned to their homes. But they left Philadelphia's Carpenters' Hall with the idea of meeting again in May of 1775 if Great Britain did not favorably respond to their demands. When the mother country refused to comply, the fuse of revolution was lit.

In March of 1775 Virginia patriots met at St. John's Church in Richmond at what was called the Second Virginia Convention. There they chose delegates to the Second Continental Congress and also debated the best course of action. Speaking at the Second Virginia Convention on March 23, 1775, Patrick Henry made what is today one of the best-loved speeches in American history. "With an unearthly fire burning in his eye" according to one witness, for twenty minutes Patrick Henry spoke of the need to fight British injustice. Then the great speaker concluded with these words:

Gentlemen may cry, peace, peace—but there is no peace. The war is actually begun! The next gale that sweeps from the north will bring to our ears the clash of resounding arms! Our brethren are already in the field! Why stand we here idle? What is it that gentlemen wish? What would they have? Is life so dear, or peace so sweet, as to be purchased at the price of chains and slavery? Forbid it, Almighty God! I know not what course others may take, but as for me, give me liberty or give me death!

Patrick Henry delivers his famous speech.

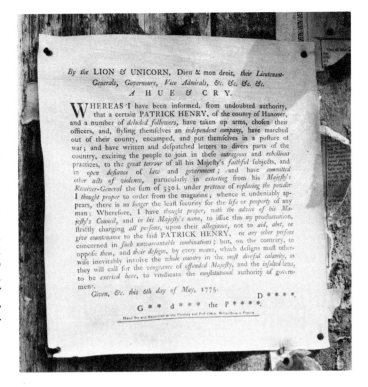

Handbill, warning the people of the Virginia Colony not to "aid, abet, or give countenance to the said Patrick Henry, or any other persons concerned in such unwarrantable combinations [taken up arms against British rule]; but, on the contrary, to oppose them, and their designs, by every means . . .", dated May 6, 1775.

This speech was so stirring that those who heard it realized it was going to be remembered as one of the great patriotic speeches of all time. One witness reported that the people in the church "looked beside themselves" with excitement at hearing these words. Another said that "Each syllable of the word 'liberty' echoed through the building. . . . His hands were open, and his arms elevated and extended; his countenance was radiant; he stood erect and defiant . . . a magnificent incarnation of Freedom." When Patrick Henry completed his speech a man named Edward Carrington, who had listened from a window just outside the church, said: "Let me be buried at this spot!" Upon his death many years later Carrington was buried very near the spot outside the church from where he had heard Patrick Henry's speech.

Patrick Henry's inspiring words helped convince the Second Virginia Convention delegates to arm their colony. American patriots also met in "Liberty Halls" and under "Liberty Trees" in the other twelve colonies to form plans for arming themselves against the British.

Less than a month after Patrick Henry said "The next gale that sweeps from the north will bring to our ears the clash of resounding arms," the fighting began. Patriots in Boston learned that British soldiers were headed toward Lexington, Massachusetts, just eleven miles northwest of Boston. The British planned to capture the patriot leaders Sam Adams and John Hancock in Lexington and then seize some gunpowder stored in nearby Concord, Massachusetts.

On the night of April 18, 1775, the Boston silversmith Paul Revere rode out to warn Sam Adams and John Hancock that the British were coming. Another rider went to Concord to warn the patriots in that town. By dawn about a

John Hancock
(1737-1793)

Samuel Adams
(1722-1803)

hundred American "minutemen" (called that because they could be ready to fight at a minute's warning) stood on the Lexington village green watching the British approach.

"Stand your ground," Captain John Parker, leader of the Lexington minutemen, is thought to have said. "Don't fire unless fired upon. But if they mean to have a war, let it begin here!"

Seeing that they were badly outnumbered, the Americans decided not to fight. But as they began to withdraw, a shot was fired—whether from the British or American side is not known. The next moment the British were shooting. Eight colonists were killed and ten were wounded in the brief Battle of Lexington on the morning of April 19, 1775. Just one British soldier was wounded.

Engraving dramatizing the midnight ride of Paul Revere

From Lexington, the British marched to nearby Concord. They burned the town hall and destroyed whatever weapons and gunpowder they could find. However, news of the massacre at Lexington had spread rapidly. Hundreds of angry patriots rushed to Concord. The Americans, who by now outnumbered the British, attacked. Hiding behind trees and farm buildings, the Americans shot at the British and chased them

Battle of Lexington, from a drawing by Hammatt Billings

all the way back to Boston. Nearly three hundred British soldiers were killed or wounded in the Battle of Concord. The Americans lost about a hundred in the running battle.

The battles at Lexington and Concord in the Massachusetts Colony marked the beginning of the revolutionary war. Just as Patrick Henry had predicted, the "clash of resounding arms" had begun north of Virginia. No one could know it yet, but Virginians were to play the leading roles in directing the American cause, and the decisive battle of the Revolution was to be fought on Virginia soil.

Independence Hall as it appeared in 1776 when the Second
Continental Congress adopted the Declaration of Independence there
on July 4

Chapter VI

The United States Is Born

Three millions of people armed in the holy cause of liberty, and in such a country as that which we possess, are invincible by any force which our enemy can send against us. . . . The battle, sir, is not to the strong alone: it is to the vigilant, the active, the brave. . . .

> *Patrick Henry, from his "Give me liberty or give me death" speech*

George Washington (1702-1799)

On May 10, 1775, just twenty-one days after the battles of Lexington and Concord, the Second Continental Congress met in Philadelphia.

One of Congress's first jobs was to select a commander in chief of the American troops. The delegates unanimously chose George Washington, who had displayed great bravery, coolheadedness, and leadership ability during the French and Indian War. "I beg it may be remembered by every gentleman in this room, that I this day declare with the utmost sincerity, I do not think myself equal to the command I am honored with," Washington said upon accepting the post. He then set out for Boston to begin training the ill-equipped and outnumbered Continental army.

On June 17, 1775, shortly before Washington's arrival in the city, the Americans and the British fought a tremendous battle near Boston. Although fought at Breed's Hill, this battle was named the Battle of Bunker Hill after a nearby hill. Twice the British charged up Breed's Hill, and twice the Americans drove them back. The Americans were outnumbered, though, and had to retreat from the third assault. The British suffered more than one thousand killed or wounded in the Battle of Bunker Hill, while the Americans had four hundred casualties. On that one day, more British officers were killed than in the entire remainder of the war. However, because the British won the hill, they were said to have won the battle.

While George Washington trained the American army, the Second Continental Congress was asserting the independence of the colonies. In June of 1776, the Virginian Richard Henry Lee introduced a resolution declaring that "These United Colonies are, and of right ought to be, free

Battle of Bunker Hill

and independent States." Several days later Congress formed a committee to write a declaration of American independence. The committee members were John Adams of Massachusetts, Benjamin Franklin of Pennsylvania, Robert R. Livingston of New York, Roger Sherman of Connecticut, and Thomas Jefferson* of Virginia.

* For more information about Thomas Jefferson see page 136

John Adams
(1735-1826)

Thomas Jefferson
(1743-1826)

Ben Franklin couldn't write the declaration because of illness and both Sherman and Livingston lacked the necessary writing ability. It was up to either John Adams or Thomas Jefferson—both future U.S. presidents—to do the job. Years later John Adams recalled the conversation that he had with Thomas Jefferson as the two men decided which of them would write the declaration:

Thomas Jefferson: "You should do it!"

John Adams: "Oh! No."

TJ: "Why will you not? You ought to do it."

JA: "I will not."

TJ: "Why?"

JA: "Reasons enough."

TJ: "What can be your reasons?"

JA: "Reason first—you are a Virginian, and a Virginian ought to appear at the head of this business. Reason second—I am obnoxious, suspected, and unpopular. You are very much otherwise. Reason third—you can write ten times better than I can."

TJ: "Well, if you are decided, I will do as well as I can."

JA: "Very well, when you have drawn it up, we will have a meeting."

There was a political reason for Adams saying that "a Virginian ought to appear at the head of this business." Some people said the Revolution was primarily Massachusetts' war against Great Britain. Key events leading to the war had occurred in Massachusetts, and the colony had also been the site of the war's first battles. John Adams and the other delegates knew that for the war to be successful people from all the colonies had to take part.

Sitting down at his desk in his apartment at Philadelphia's Market and Seventh streets,

Painting by N.C. Wyeth recalls a young Thomas Jefferson drafting the Declaration of Independence.

Part of the rough draft of the Declaration of Independence handwritten by Jefferson

Thomas Jefferson started writing. "When in the course of human events it becomes necessary for one people to dissolve the political bands which have connected them with another . . ." he began. Thomas Jefferson wrote the declaration in two weeks in late June of 1776. Amazingly, he used no reference books, but instead blended his own thoughts and phrases with ones he had encountered in his widespread reading.

When Jefferson showed his great document, the Declaration of Independence, to the other men on

The signing of the Declaration of Independence
(W.L. Ormsby, engraver)

the committee, they suggested a few minor
changes. On July 2, Congress discussed the
declaration, and then adopted it on July 4 after
making a few more changes. July 4, 1776, the day
the Declaration of Independence was adopted, is
generally considered the day the United States
was born. Of the fifty-six members of the
Continental Congress who signed the

Declaration, seven were from Virginia. They were George Wythe, Richard Henry Lee, Thomas Jefferson, Benjamin Harrison, Thomas Nelson, Jr., Francis Lightfoot Lee, and Carter Braxton.

In the Declaration of Independence, the term "united States of America" was used to describe the rebelling colonies. As far as the American patriots were concerned, Connecticut, Delaware, Georgia, Maryland, Massachusetts, New Hampshire, New Jersey, New York, North Carolina, Pennsylvania, Rhode Island, South Carolina, and Virginia were no longer colonies, but part of a new country. To make this a reality, however, the Americans first had to win a war against the most powerful nation on earth.

Portraits of the men who signed the Declaration of Independence

Opposite page: Copy of the Declaration of Independence

IN CONGRESS, JULY 4, 1776

The unanimous Declaration of the thirteen united States of America.

Heroic portrait of a revolutionary soldier in uniform filling his gun from his powder horn

Today many Americans picture the Continental army as liberty-loving soldiers who fearlessly followed their beloved general, George Washington. Many also think that all Americans supported the Revolution. This wasn't the case. The ragtag Continental army continually suffered from disagreements and desertions. Some Americans sided with the British. Others supported the war, but thought George Washington was doing a poor job.

Patriots pull down the statue of George III in a New York City park.

Patriots ride a Tory, a person loyal to the king of England, out of town on a rail.

At the war's start, about three fourths of the American colonists were Whigs—people who favored independence from Great Britain. About one-fourth sided with Britain and were called Tories, or Loyalists. The Tories tended to be wealthier people who had invested large sums of money in business dealings with Great Britain. They sometimes spied on the Americans and informed the British of their plans.

But the Tories were only one of the problems facing George Washington. Unlike the well-trained and well-equipped British soldiers,

TO ALL BRAVE, HEALTHY, ABLE BODIED, AND WELL DISPOSED YOUNG MEN,

IN THIS NEIGHBOURHOOD, WHO HAVE ANY INCLINATION TO JOIN THE TROOPS,

NOW RAISING UNDER

GENERAL WASHINGTON,

FOR THE DEFENCE OF THE

LIBERTIES AND INDEPENDENCE

OF THE UNITED STATES,

Againſt the hoſtile deſigns of foreign enemies,

TAKE NOTICE,

THAT .... tuesday, wednsday thursday friday and saturday at Spotswood in

Middlesex .... county, attendance will be given by Lieutenant Recuting .... with his muſic and recruiting party of .... company in Major Shute's Battalion of the 11th regiment of infantry, commanded by Lieutenant Colonel Aaron Ogden, for the purpoſe of receiving the enrollment of ſuch youth of SPIRIT, as may be willing to enter into this HONOURABLE ſervice.

The ENCOURAGEMENT at this time, to enliſt, is truly liberal and generous, namely, a bounty of TWELVE dollars, an annual and fully ſufficient ſupply of good and handſome cloathing, a daily allowance of a large and ample ration of proviſions, together with SIXTY dollars a year in GOLD and SILVER money on account of pay, the whole of which the ſoldier may lay up for himſelf and friends, as all articles proper for his ſubſiſtance and comfort are provided by law, without any expence to him.

Thoſe who may favour this recruiting party with their attendance as above, will have an opportunity of hearing and ſeeing in a more particular manner, the great advantages which theſe brave men will have, who ſhall embrace this opportunity of ſpending a few happy years in viewing the different parts of this beautiful continent, in the honourable and truly reſpectable character of a ſoldier, after which, he may, if he pleaſes return home to his friends, with his pockets FULL of money and his head COVERED with laurels.

GOD SAVE THE UNITED STATES.

Recruiting poster for General Washington's Continental army seeks volunteers willing to fight for the "liberties and independence of the United States against the hostile designs of foreign enemies." The poster lists the advantages of joining the army as follows: "The encouragement at this time to enlist is truly liberal and generous, namely, a bounty of twelve dollars, an annual and fully sufficient supply of good and handsome cloathing, a daily allowance of a large and ample ration of provisions, together with sixty dollars a year in gold and silver money on account of pay, the whole of which the soldier may lay up for himself and friends, as all articles proper for his subsistance and comfort are provided by law, without any expense to him.

"Those who may favor this recruiting party with their attendance as above, will have an opportunity of hearing and seeing in a more particular manner, the great advantages which these brave men will have who shall embrace this opportunity of spending a few happy years in viewing the different parts of this beautiful continent, in the honourable and truly respectable character of a soldier, after which, he may, if he pleases return home to his friends, with his pockets full of money and his head covered with laurels ... God Save the United States"

Washington's Continental army was a sorry mess throughout most of the war. The soldiers had no uniforms (and, except for the officers, would still have none even at the war's end), not enough weapons, and little discipline. Many of the soldiers signed up for periods that ended on a certain date, such as December 31 or November 30. This meant that Washington had to plan his attacks around these deadlines. There were also mass desertions. When they became distressed at their situation, didn't feel like fighting anymore, or wanted to go home for the harvest, some soldiers would simply take off. Had the American leaders tried to punish the deserters, the entire army might have quit on them.

The fact was that often the soldiers couldn't be blamed for deserting. Much of the time the Continental Congress couldn't raise enough money to feed them decently or even pay them. When the men were paid, it was with the nearly worthless Continental paper dollars first issued by Congress in 1776. So unreliable was this money that when the American people of 1776 wanted to say something was worthless, they

Lost for over a hundred years, this portrait of a black revolutionary war sailor was discovered in 1976. It is believed that the man was a member of the 20-gun privateer *General Washington*, the ship that appears in the background of the full-sized painting.

would exclaim, "It's not worth a Continental!"

Of all the problems facing George Washington, the one that bothered him most was the impossibility of fighting a big battle against the British. If Washington had attempted it, the small American army would have been slaughtered and the war would have quickly ended. Had this happened, children in what is now the United States might be taught that George Washington was the worst traitor the British Empire has ever known instead of "The Father of His Country."

Instead of a big open battle, George Washington counted heavily on raids. One of the most successful of these raids was made at Trenton, New Jersey on December 26, 1776. Early that morning the Hessians (German soldiers fighting for pay on the British side) were in Trenton sleeping off the effects of their Christmas celebration. Suddenly Washington's men attacked. The Americans lost just a few men in the Battle of Trenton, but the Hessians had one hundred killed and wounded and about twelve hundred taken prisoner.

Besides Trenton, the Americans won battles at Princeton (1777) in New Jersey, Bennington

General Washington crosses the Delaware River.

(1777) at the Vermont-New York border, and
Freeman's Farm (1777) in New York. However,
they lost other important battles at Long Island
(1776) in New York and Brandywine (1777) in
Pennsylvania.

The low point for the Continental army came in
December of 1777 when Washington and his
11,000-man army took up winter quarters at
Valley Forge, Pennsylvania. By this time the

Washington and Lafayette, the young French nobleman who gave money to support the American cause, visit the cold and hungry troops at Valley Forge.

Continental army had so little food and clothing that it appeared the soldiers would soon have to surrender. George Washington wrote that "you might have trailed the army . . . to Valley Forge by the blood of their feet" because many of the men didn't even have shoes.

General Washington ordered his men to build huts, which served as their homes during that terrible winter at Valley Forge. Washington promised his men that he would help them the best he could, but the Continental Congress lacked the money to provide the desperately needed aid. Each day during that winter of 1777-78, dozens of American soldiers died from hunger, disease, and cold.

Wooden houses sheltered the troops at Valley Forge during the winter of 1777-78.

To make things worse, George Washington was receiving heavy criticism during those dark days. He was being called a "weak General," "damnably deficient," and worse. Even members of the Continental Congress were saying that General Horatio Gates or Major General Charles Lee would do a better job than Washington. Hungry for a major victory, Americans could not understand why Washington avoided big battles. So upset was Washington by these criticisms that on December 23, 1777, he fired off a letter to the Continental Congress in which he angrily said:

> *I can assure those Gentlemen [those who criticized the army for not attacking] that it is a much easier and less distressing thing to draw remonstrances in a comfortable room by a good fire side than to occupy a cold bleak hill and sleep under frost and snow without Cloaths or Blankets; however, though they seem to have little feeling for the naked and distressed soldier, I feel super-abundantly for them, and from my soul I pity those miseries, which it is neither in my power to relieve or prevent.*

In this same letter written from Valley Forge the heartbroken commander in chief said that, unless some major changes occurred, the army would soon have to "starve, dissolve, or disperse." He also explained—as he was to do so often during this period—that he just didn't have enough men to make a major attack.

Had the British attacked the Americans at Valley Forge, they could have wiped out most of the army. But the British were sure that they could win the war any time they chose. Finishing off the helpless Americans holed up at Valley Forge would have looked bad in the eyes of the world.

Ragged soldier stands guard at Valley Forge.

By spring of 1778, more than one quarter of the eleven thousand American soldiers at Valley Forge had died. But then came some good news for the Americans. In February of 1778 an old enemy of Great Britain, France, entered the war on the American side. The French supplied soldiers, sailors, ships, weapons, and money to the American cause.

French aid helped turn the tide in favor of the colonists, who began winning important battles on both land and sea. Several Virginians played key roles in the American victories. George Rogers Clark (1752-1818), who had been born near Charlottesville, Virginia, led the Americans to victory at Kaskaskia, Illinois in 1778 and Vincennes, Indiana in 1779. The great Virginia cavalry officer Henry ("Light-Horse Harry") Lee* commanded the Americans in their victorious raid of the British fort at Paulus Hook (now Jersey City), New Jersey in August of 1779. Brigadier General Daniel Morgan (1736-1802), who had moved to Virginia from New Jersey as a youth, led the Americans to victory at Cowpens, South Carolina in January of 1781.

"Light-Horse Harry" Lee

Although no major battles were waged in Virginia until the end of the war, the colony suffered tremendous damage from British forces. In 1779 British naval forces captured Portsmouth, Virginia. They burned the nearby town of Suffolk, and sent out raiding parties which damaged or destroyed other nearby towns. In January of 1781 British forces entered Richmond, looted Virginia's capital, and burned several important buildings. What hurt especially was that the British troops in Richmond were led by Benedict Arnold, a former American general who had recently turned traitor and had joined the British side.

Meanwhile, George Washington's army was

* For more information about Henry ("Light-Horse Harry") Lee see page 138

The Siege of Yorktown

growing in numbers, supplies, and confidence. By 1781 Washington could start planning the major battle he had wanted to fight against the British ever since he'd become commander in chief in 1775. Washington very much wanted to capture New York City, which the British had held since 1776. However, two events shifted his attention to Virginia. First, in summer of 1781 the British General Charles Cornwallis led his army of about eight thousand men into the little tobacco port of

Yorktown, Virginia. Second, Washington had been told by the French that they would be sending a large fleet into Chesapeake Bay in fall of 1781. Washington figured that his soldiers on land combined with the French sailors on the sea could surround the large British army at Yorktown.

In late September of 1781 Washington led his army of approximately seventeen thousand men to Yorktown. Like a slowly tightening noose, the Americans and the French closed in on the British. In early October, Washington's soldiers began firing on the British with their cannons and other heavy guns from their positions outside Yorktown. Day and night they pounded the British defenses until the ground in and around Yorktown was pockmarked with craters from the heavy fire. James Thacher, an American army doctor, described the deadly bombardment:

Map of the Yorktown area

> . . . all around was thunder and lightening from our numerous cannon and mortars. . . . Some of our shells, overreaching the town, are seen to fall into the river, and bursting, throw up columns of water, like the spouting of the monsters of the deep.

Dr. Thacher also said that at night the heavy shelling lit up the sky as if it were filled with meteors, and that "the whole peninsula trembles" from the continuous firing.

The British returned the fire as best they could, but they lacked the big guns and position to put up much of a fight. About six hundred British (and about one hundred American) soldiers had already been killed in the bombardment and fighting. Realizing that all his men might be killed unless he gave up, on October 17, 1781, General Cornwallis sent this historic letter to George Washington:

Letter Cornwallis wrote to Washington on October 17, 1781:

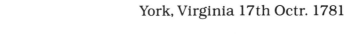

York, Virginia 17th Octr. 1781

Sir

I propose a cessation of hostilities for twenty four hours, and that two officers may be appointed by each side to meet at Mr. Moore's house to settle terms for the surrender of the posts of York and Gloucester. I have the honour to be

Sir

Your most obedient and
His Excellency   most humble servant
    General Washington   Cornwallis

George Washington answered Cornwallis's message by saying that he had "An Ardent Desire to spare the further Effusion of Blood." The two generals worked out the terms of the British surrender. Then, on October 19, 1781, as their bands played "The World Turned Upside Down"

British surrender at Yorktown. General Cornwallis is shown at right handing over his sword. General Washington stands at the left.

and other tunes, the British marched out to surrender. A Virginia soldier who witnessed this scene described it like this:

The British troops marched out of Yorktown in solid columns, between the lines of the American army into an old field, where they deposted first their drums with the fifes on the heads of the drums, struck their colors into the soil, laid their guns on the ground, faced about and marched back into Yorktown.

Charles, Earl Cornwallis, after an engraving published in 1784

The Americans were quiet during the British surrender. But once the British were back inside

Yorktown with their American guards, George Washington's army began to celebrate. One American colonel described the celebration scene as follows:

I noticed that the officers and soldiers could scarcely talk for laughing and they could scarcely walk for jumping and dancing and singing....

The British surrender at Yorktown on October 19, 1781, marked the end of major revolutionary war fighting. On September 3, 1783, the war formally ended when the U.S. and Great Britain signed a peace treaty, and on November 25, 1783, the last of the British soldiers left New York City. The American patriots—with the help from the French—had won a war that for so long they hadn't seemed capable of winning. A new country, the United States of America, now took its place among the nations of the world!

The new country was beset by problems. For one thing, each separate state was like a little country of its own. The U.S. was loosely held together under an agreement called the Articles of Confederation, which the Continental Congress had approved in 1781. However, the Articles gave little authority to the Congress. The Congress had

The last boatload of British troops leaves New York, 1783.

no treasury. Each state printed its own money. The Congress had only a tiny army at its disposal and no way to make the states pay taxes. It did not even have a permanent home. Congress moved about among such cities as Philadelphia, Princeton (New Jersey), Annapolis (Maryland), and New York City.

Whenever an emergency arose, the Congress couldn't respond properly. One event that demonstrated this was Shays' Rebellion, an insurrection of western Massachusetts farmers which lasted from September of 1786 until February of 1787. The Congress didn't have enough men to put down this rebellion, so Massachusetts militia had to do it.

In May of 1787 George Washington, who had become a national hero upon the British surrender at Yorktown, described the government's sorry situation in a letter to Thomas Jefferson:

> *. . . the situation of the General Government (if it can be called a governmt.) is shaken to the foundation, and liable to be overset by every blast. In a word, it is at an end, and unless a remedy is soon applied, anarchy and confusion will inevitably ensue.*

James Madison
(1751-1836)

A "remedy" was "soon applied." In spring of 1787 a Constitutional Convention met in Philadelphia. The delegates at this convention created a new set of governing laws for the nation: the Constitution of the United States. It was written in spring and summer of 1787, largely under the direction of the Virginian James Madison (1751-1836), who is called "The Father of the Constitution." The Constitution gave much more power to the national government than had the Articles of Confederation, and this greatly strengthened the country. The United States is governed by the Constitution to this day.

When Delaware ratified the Constitution on December 7, 1787, it became the first state. Virginia, which had been the site of the first permanent English settlement in America, the home of Powhatan, Pocahontas, John Smith, and George Washington, and the scene of the final revolutionary war battle, became the tenth state when it ratified the Constitution on June 25, 1788.

The Liberty Bell

GEORGE WASHINGTON (1732-1799)

Born on February 22, 1732, in Westmoreland County, Virginia, George Washington grew up on several plantations in the eastern part of the colony. Little is known about his education except that he spent only about seven years in school. He studied reading, handwriting, and his favorite subject, arithmetic. A tall, athletic boy, Washington loved to ride his horse or hunt in the woods when he was not in school or doing his farm chores.

When Washington was fourteen he wanted to join the British navy, but his mother would not let him. His second choice was to become a surveyor, a person who maps land and boundaries and land formations. At fifteen Washington went to work as an assistant surveyor. By the time he was seventeen he was helping to map out the town of Alexandria, Virginia, and had been appointed the official surveyor of Virginia's Culpeper County. Washington spent his earnings on land and he had eighteen hundred acres of his own by the age of eighteen.

About the time that twenty-year-old George Washington inherited the lovely plantation called Mount Vernon, he started his military career. At this time the British were ready to wage war against the French and the Indians. Appointed as a major in the Virginia militia, Washington was soon in the thick of the fighting. He wrote of one French and Indian War battle: "I luckily escaped without a wound, though I had four bullets through my coat and two horses shot under me."

In early 1759, shortly after he resigned from the British colonial army, Washington married Martha Dandridge Custis. For the next fifteen years, Washington worked on business deals, attended balls and dinners, and went on fox hunts as did Virginia's other wealthy plantation owners.

This happy way of life ended when the colonists asked Washington to lead them during their troubles with the British. Washington was elected as a delegate to the two Continental Congresses, and the delegates of the Second Congress chose him as commander in chief of the Continental army. During the difficult times when it seemed that the Continental army could not possibly win, Washington kept his men from giving up.

After the war was won, Washington was so popular with his countrymen that many wanted to make him king. "No greater mischief could happen to our country," Washington responded. When Americans decided to elect a president instead, George Washington was the overwhelming winner. While serving as the first president of the United States from 1789 to 1797, Washington helped keep the states from fighting with each other and also helped our country earn the respect of the other nations of the world.

Washington is remembered today as "The Father of His Country." Our nation's capital, Washington, D.C., is named for him, as is the state of Washington and many counties and towns in the United States. Because Washington meant so much to the United States in its early years, his friend "Light-Horse Harry" Lee said this about our first president shortly after his death:

> First in war, first in peace, and first in the hearts of his countrymen.

PATRICK HENRY (1736-1799)

Early in his life it appeared that Patrick Henry, who was born on a plantation in Hanover County, Virginia, would be the family ne'er-do-well. The second of eleven children, Henry went to work as a clerk for a merchant at the age of fifteen. The following year, he and his older brother set up their own store, but it failed. Even though he had little money, Henry got married at age eighteen and began to farm. He was as poor a farmer as he was a storekeeper. In fact, for a while it appeared that the only thing Henry was good for was for having children. Over the years, he and his two wives had sixteen of them!

After his farming troubles, Henry tried to set up another store, but this failed also. Having no other ideas of what to do, Henry moved his family to his father-in-law's tavern. He worked at the tavern as a part-time barkeeper and also entertained the guests by playing the fiddle.

At twenty-four, Henry realized that he had to make something of himself, so he decided to become a lawyer. After just six weeks of study he went to Williamsburg to take his bar examination. Although Henry did not know many details of law, the examiners passed him because of his quick mind and smooth tongue.

Even though he said *larnin'* instead of *learning* and *nateral* instead of *natural*, Henry became a successful lawyer who thrilled people with his speeches. People also liked the young lawyer because he was a straightforward man who enjoyed the simple pleasures of life, such as playing the fiddle and hunting. Thomas Jefferson once described how Henry spent the winter when the courts were not in session:

> He would make up a party of poor hunters of his neighborhood, go off with them to the piny woods of Fluvanna, and pass weeks in hunting deer, of which he was passionately fond, sleeping under a tent, before a fire, wearing the same shirt the whole time, and covering all the dirt of his dress with a hunting shirt.

Henry's success as a lawyer helped him win election to the Virginia House of Burgesses in 1764. There he became known as a young firebrand who spoke out passionately against what he thought to be British tyranny.

In the summer of 1774 Henry was elected as a delegate from Virginia to the First Continental Congress. The delegates to the Congress argued so much that John Adams once said they would not be able to agree that three plus two equals five. Henry was a unifying force among the delegates, especially when he made his "I am not a Virginian, but an American!" speech. The following year, while addressing Virginia patriots in Richmond, Henry made his great "Give me liberty or give me death!" speech.

Henry's stirring words helped him win election as the first non-British governor of Virginia. Henry served twice as Virginia governor, from 1776 to 1779 and again from 1784 to 1786. In an age in which most politicians were snobbish toward ordinary people, Governor Henry became beloved and admired by the Virginians by being the first U.S. politician to call his supporters "my fellow citizens." In the late 1780s, Henry helped promote the adoption of the Bill of Rights, which is made up of the first ten amendments to the United States Constitution. The greatest orator of the American Revolution died shortly after winning election to the Virginia state legislature.

THOMAS JEFFERSON (1743-1826)

Thomas Jefferson was born at Shadwell, his father's plantation in central Virginia's Albemarle County, which was then at the edge of the wilderness. His first fourteen years were evenly divided between Shadwell, where his neighbors were mostly poor farmers, and a large Tidewater estate called Tuckahoe, which his father, Peter, managed for a friend.

While living in the Tidewater region, Jefferson learned to dance minuets, play the violin, and conduct himself like a proper English gentleman. Out in the wilderness he spent many happy hours swimming and fishing in the Rivanna River, hunting and riding in the forest, and studying the plants, animals, and Indian burial mounds of the countryside with his father. No matter where the red-haired boy was, he spent much of his time reading his father's books written by Shakespeare, Swift, and other authors.

When Jefferson was fourteen years old his happy life was shattered when his father died. As the oldest son, Thomas inherited Shadwell, which by then consisted of more than twenty-five hundred acres of land and several dozen slaves. While his guardian managed the estate, Jefferson attended the College of William and Mary, where he amazed his professors with his thirst for knowledge. At night, when the other young men went off to the tavern, Jefferson would stay up studying astronomy, mathematics, law, music, history, religion, and politics.

After his graduation from college at age nineteen, Jefferson became a very successful lawyer. At only twenty-six years of age he was elected to Virginia's House of Burgesses. While serving as a burgess he spoke out on the colonists' right to free themselves from Great Britain. This was one reason why he was chosen as a delegate to the Second Continental Congress in 1775. The brilliant Virginian wrote the Declaration of Independence in seventeen days in June of 1776. Ever since its adoption on July 4, 1776, the Declaration has been the best-loved document in United States history.

Jefferson continued to serve his country for half a century after penning the Declaration. Between 1779 and 1793 he served as governor of Virginia, United States minister to France, and then the first United States secretary of state under President Washington. From 1797 to 1801 he served as vice-president of the United States. Elected in 1801, Jefferson became the third president of the United States, an office he held until 1809. During Jefferson's presidency the Louisiana Purchase was made, doubling the size of the United States. Jefferson also kept our country out of war during difficult times.

Jefferson often said, "It is wonderful how much may be done if we are always doing." Following his own advice, Jefferson found time for much more than politics during his long life. The greatest American-born architect of his time, Jefferson designed the University of Virginia, the Virginia Capitol, and his famous home, Monticello (which can be seen on the back of the Jefferson nickel). A strong believer in education, he founded the University of Virginia in 1819. At a time when only the wealthy were able to attend school, Jefferson was the first well-known American to champion the cause of public education. He opposed slavery when most wealthy white Southerners favored it. Jefferson also was an amateur scientist (nicknamed "Mr. Mammoth" because of his prehistoric bones collection), an outstanding concert violinist, and the inventor of the first swivel chair. Finally, Jefferson's library, containing more than six thousand books, became the basis for our country's Library of Congress.

For all these accomplishments, the author of the Declaration of Independence is remembered as one of the most remarkable Americans who ever lived. Thomas Jefferson died at the age of eighty-three on July 4, 1826, fifty years to the day after the Declaration of Independence was adopted and the same day that John Adams died.

HENRY ("LIGHT-HORSE HARRY") LEE (1756-1818)

Born at Leesylvania, his family's plantation in Prince William County, Virginia, Henry Lee showed at an early age that he had the makings of both a soldier and a scholar. He learned to ride a horse at age three or four, and, by the age of eight, he was amazing his father's friend, George Washington, with his riding ability. At that age Henry also surprised visitors by greeting them in perfect Latin.

At fourteen Henry entered the College of New Jersey (now Princeton University), where he and his friends James Madison and Aaron Burr studied such subjects as Latin, Greek, Hebrew, philosophy, science, history, and law. Although he was a fine scholar, Henry was known to take time out from his eighteen-hour college day to explode gunpowder in his classmates' rooms and to go atop the college's Nassau Hall, where he would look through a telescope at the pretty girls in the neighborhood!

When Harry (as he was now called) graduated from college at age seventeen, there was talk of war between the American colonists and Great Britain. Harry, who already was well known for his skill with horse, sword, and pistol, dreamed of helping the colonies win their freedom. Hoping to join the cavalry (horse soldiers) in case of war, he galloped around Leesylvania for hours each day while slashing at targets he hung from tree branches.

In the summer of 1776 Harry was made a captain in the cavalry and was allowed to recruit his own soldiers for his unit, the Fifth Troop. In the early stages of the war Harry Lee helped feed George Washington's Continental army by making food raids on the British. So fast and daring was Lee that he earned the nickname "Light-Horse Harry."

In 1778 "Light-Horse Harry" was promoted to major and was named commander of a troop that became known as "Lee's Legion." The following year, "Light-Horse Harry" thought up a daring plan for a raid on the British fort at Paulus Hook (now Jersey City), New Jersey. After George Washington approved of the plan, Lee gathered his troops near the fort in mid-August.

At three o'clock, on the morning of August 19, 1779, "Light-Horse Harry" led several hundred men in a surprise attack on the British fort. Lee's forces captured almost four hundred prisoners while suffering only one death and two men wounded in the fighting. This victory helped earn Lee the reputation as the American Revolution's greatest cavalryman.

"Light-Horse Harry" Lee had other great moments during the Revolution, and by the time the British surrendered at Yorktown he was a national hero. After the war he served as Virginia's governor from 1791 to 1794 and served in the U.S. House of Representatives from 1799 to 1801. In 1812 "Light-Horse Harry" Lee suffered severe wounds while trying to protect a newspaper publisher from an angry mob in Baltimore. He never recovered from his wounds, and he died several years later. "Light-Horse Harry" was the father of Robert E. Lee, the Confederate general who was one of the greatest military leaders in United States history.

Five of the first nine presidents of the United States were born in colonial Virginia. The five were George Washington, Thomas Jefferson, James Madison, James Monroe, and William Henry Harrison. Because eventually the total of Virginia-born presidents reached eight (the other three being John Tyler, Zachary Taylor, and Woodrow Wilson), the state is nicknamed the *Mother of Presidents* today.

George Washington, president of the United States 1789-1796; Thomas Jefferson, president of the United States 1801-1809; James Madison, president of the United States 1809-1817; James Monroe, president of the United States 1817-1825

William Henry Harrison, president of the United States 1841; John Tyler, president of the United States 1841-1845; Zachary Taylor, president of the United States 1849-1850; Woodrow Wilson, president of the United States 1913-1921

RESOLUTION OF SECRECY ADOPTED BY THE CONTINENTAL CONGRESS, NOVEMBER 9, 1775

Resolved, That every member of this Congress considers himself under the ties of virtue, honour, and love of his country, not to divulge, directly or indirectly, any matter or thing agitated or debated in Congress, before the same shall have been determined, without leave of the Congress; nor any matter or thing determined in Congress, which a majority of the Congress shall order to be kept secret. And that if any member shall violate this agreement, he shall be expelled this Congress, and deemed an enemy to the liberties of America, and liable to be treated as such; and that every member signify his consent to this agreement by signing the same.

On August 23, 1775 George III signed this proclamation for the suppression of rebellion in the colonies.

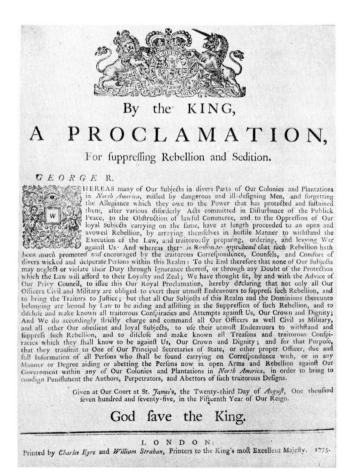

PREAMBLE AND RESOLUTION OF THE VIRGINIA CONVENTION, MAY 15, 1776, INSTRUCTING THE VIRGINIA DELEGATES IN THE CONTINENTAL CONGRESS TO "PROPOSE TO THAT RESPECTABLE BODY TO DECLARE THE UNITED COLONIES FREE AND INDEPENDENT STATES"

Forasmuch as all the endeavours of the United Colonies, by the most decent representations and petitions to the King and Parliament of *Great Britain*, to restore peace and security to *America* under the *British* Government, and a reunion with that people upon just and liberal terms, instead of a redress of grievances, have produced, from an imperious and vindictive Administration, increased insult, oppression, and a vigorous attempt to effect our total destruction:—By a late act all these Colonies are declared to be in rebellion, and out of the protection of the *British* Crown, our properties subjected to confiscation, our people, when captivated, compelled to join in the murder and plunder of their relations and countrymen, and all former rapine and oppression of *Americans* declared legal and just; fleets and armies are raised, and the aid of foreign troops engaged to assist these destructive purposes; the King's representative in this Colony hath not only withheld all the powers of Government from operating for our safety, but, having retired on board an armed ship, is carrying on a piratical and savage war against us, tempting our slaves by every artifice to resort to him, and training and employing them against their masters. In this state of extreme danger, we have no alternative left but an abject submission to the will of those overbearing tyrants, or a total separation from the Crown and Government of *Great Britain*, uniting and exerting the strength af all *America* for defence, and forming alliances with foreign Powers for commerce and aid in war:—Wherefore, appealing to the Searcher of hearts for the sincerity of former declarations expressing our desire to preserve the connection with that nation, and that we are driven from that inclination by their wicked councils, and the eternal law of self-preservation:

Resolved, unanimously, That the Delegates appointed to represent this Colony in General Congress be instructed to propose to that respectable body to declare the United Colonies free and independent States, absolved from all allegiance to, or dependence upon, the Crown or Parliament of *Great Britain*; and that they give the assent of this Colony to such declaration, and to whatever measures may be thought proper and necessary by the Congress for forming foreign alliances, and a Confederation of the Colonies, at such time and in the manner as to them shall seem best: *Provided*, That the power of forming Government for, and the regulations of the internal concerns of each Colony, be left to the respective Colonial Legislatures.

Resolved, unanimously, That a Committee be appointed to prepare a Declaration of Rights, and such a plan of Government as will be most likely to maintain peace and order in this Colony, and secure substantial and equal liberty to the people.

And a Committee was appointed of the following gentlemen: Mr. Archibald Cary, Mr. Meriwether Smith, Mr. Mercer, Mr. Henry Lee, Mr. Treasurer, Mr. Henry, Mr. Dandridge, Mr. Edmund Randolph, Mr. Gilmer, Mr. Bland, Mr. Digges, Mr. Carrington, Mr. Thomas Ludwell Lee, Mr. Cabell, Mr. Jones, Mr. Blair, Mr. Fleming, Mr. Tazewell, Mr. Richard Cary, Mr. Bullitt, Mr. Watts, Mr. Banister, Mr. Page, Mr. Starke, Mr. David Mason, Mr. Adams, Mr. Read, and Mr. Thomas Lewis.

RESOLUTION INTRODUCED IN THE CONTINENTAL CONGRESS BY RICHARD HENRY LEE (VA.) PROPOSING A DECLARATION OF INDEPENDENCE, JUNE 7, 1776

Resolved, That these United Colonies are, and of right ought to be, free and independent States that they are absolved from all allegiance to the British Crown, and that all political connection between them and the State of Great Britain is, and ought to be, totally dissolved.

That it is expedient forthwith to take the most effectual measures for forming foreign Alliances.

That a plan of confederation be prepared and transmitted to the respective Colonies for their consideration and approbation.

The declaration of rights was issued on June 12, 1776 by the Convention of Delegates at the capitol in Williamsburg.

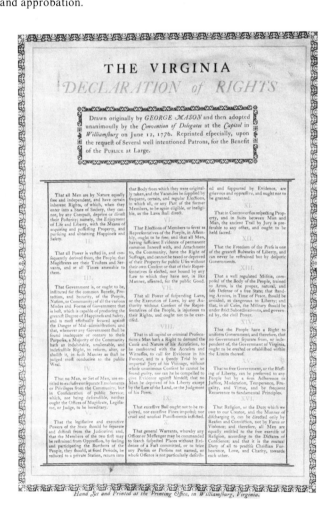

THE DECLARATION OF INDEPENDENCE—1776

In Congress, July 4, 1776

THE UNANIMOUS DECLARATION OF THE THIRTEEN
UNITED STATES OF AMERICA

When in the Course of human events, it becomes necessary for one people to dissolve the political bands which have connected them with another, and to assume among the powers of the earth, the separate and equal station to which the Laws of Nature and of Nature's God entitle them, a decent respect to the opinions of mankind requires that they should declare the causes which impel them to the separation.—We hold these truths to be self-evident, that all men are created equal, that they are endowed by their Creator with certain unalienable Rights, that among these are Life, Liberty and the pursuit of Happiness.—That to secure these just rights, Governments are instituted among Men, deriving their just powers from the consent of the governed,—That whenever any Form of Government becomes destructive of these ends, it is the Right of the People to alter or to abolish it, and to institute new Government, laying its foundation on such principles and organizing its powers in such form, as to them shall seem most likely to effect their Safety and Happiness. Prudence, indeed, will dictate that Governments long established should not be changed for light and transient causes; and accordingly all experience hath shown, that mankind are more disposed to suffer, while evils are sufferable, than to right themselves by abolishing the forms to which they are accustomed. But when a long train of abuses and usurpations, pursuing invariably the same Object evinces a design to reduce them under absolute Despotism, it is their right, it is their duty, to throw off such Government, and to provide new Guards for their future security.—Such has been the patient sufferance of these Colonies; and such is now the necessity which constrains them to alter their former Systems of Government. The history of the present King of Great Britain is a history of repeated injuries and usurpations, all having in direct object the establishment of an absolute Tyranny over these States. To prove this, let Facts be submitted to a candid world.—He has refused his Assent to Laws, the most wholesome and necessary for the public good.—He has forbidden his Governors to pass Laws of immediate and pressing importance, unless suspended in their operation till his Assent should be obtained; and when so suspended, he has utterly neglected to attend to them.—He has refused to pass other Laws for the accommodation of large districts of people, unless those people would relinquish the right of Representation in the Legislature, a right inestimable to them and formidable to tyrants only.—He has called together legislative bodies at places unusual, uncomfortable, and distant from the depository of their public Records, for the sole purpose of fatiguing them into compliance with his measures.—He has dissolved Representative Houses repeatedly, for opposing with manly firmness his invasions on the rights of the people.—He has refused for a long time, after such dissolutions, to cause others to be elected; whereby the Legislative powers, incapable of Annihilation, have returned to the People at large for their exercise; the State remaining in the mean time exposed to all the dangers of invasion from without, and convulsions within.—He has endeavoured to prevent the population of these States; for that purpose obstructing the Laws for Naturalization of Foreigners; refusing to pass others to encourage their migration hither, and raising the conditions of new Appropriations of Lands.—He has obstructed the Administration of Justice, by refusing his Assent to Laws for establishing Judiciary powers.—He has made Judges dependent on his Will alone, for the tenure of their offices, and the amount and payment of their salaries.—He has erected a multitude of New Offices, and sent hither swarms of Officers to harrass our people, and eat out their substance.—He has kept among us, in times of peace, Standing Armies, without the Consent of our legislatures.—He has affected to render the Military independent of and superior to the Civil power.—He has combined with others to subject us to a jurisdiction foreign to our constitution, and unacknowledged by our laws; giving his Assent to their Acts of pretended Legislation:—For quartering large bodies of armed troops among us:—For protecting them, by a mock Trial, from punishment for any Murders which they should commit on the Inhabitants of these States:—For cutting off our Trade with all parts of the world:—For imposing Taxes on us without our Consent:—For depriving us in many cases, of the benefits of Trial by Jury:—For transporting us beyond Seas to be tried for pretended offences:—For abolishing the free System of English Laws in a neighbouring Province, establishing therein an Arbitrary government, and enlarging its Boundaries so as to render it at once an example and fit instrument for introducing the same absolute rule into these Colonies:—For taking away our Charters, abolishing our most valuable Laws, and altering fundamentally the Forms of our Governments:—For suspending our own Legislatures, and declaring themselves invested with power to legislate for us in all cases whatsoever.—He has abdicated Government here, by declaring us out of his Protection and waging War against us.—He has plundered our seas, ravaged our Coasts, burnt our towns, and destroyed the lives of our people.—He is at this time transporting large Armies of foreign Mercenaries to compleat the works of death, desolation and tyranny, already begun with circumstances of Cruelty & perfidy scarcely parallelled in the most barbarous ages, and totally unworthy the Head of a civilized nation.—He has constrained our fellow Citizens taken Captive on the high Seas to bear Arms against their Country, to become the executioners of their friends and Brethren, or to fall themselves by their Hands.— He has excited domestic insurrections amongst us, and has endeavoured to bring on the inhabitants of our frontiers, the merciless Indian Savages, whose known rule of warfare, is an indistinguished destruction of all ages, sexes and conditions. In every stage of these Oppressions We have Petitioned for Redress in the most humble terms: Our repeated Petitions have been answered only by repeated injury. A Prince, whose character is thus marked by every act which may define a Tyrant, is unfit to be the ruler of a free people. Nor have We been wanting in attentions to our Brittish brethren. We have warned them from time to time of attempts by their legislature to extend an unwarrantable jurisdiction over us. We have reminded them of the circumstances of our emigration and settlement here. We have appealed to their native justice and magnanimity, and we have conjured them by the ties of our common kindred to disavow these usurpations, which, would inevitably interrupt our connections and correspondence. They too have been deaf to the voice of justice and of consanguinity. We must, therefore, acquiesce in the necessity, which denounces our Separation, and hold them, as we hold the rest of mankind, Enemies in War, in Peace Friends.—

WE, THEREFORE, THE REPRESENTATIVES OF THE UNITED STATES OF AMERICA, in General Congress, Assembled, appealing to the Supreme Judge of the world for the rectitude of our intentions, do, in the Name, and by Authority of the good People of these Colonies, solemnly publish and declare, That these United Colonies are, and of Right ought to be FREE AND INDEPENDENT STATES; that they are Absolved from all Allegiance to the British Crown, and that all political connection between them and the State of Great Britain, is and ought to be totally dissolved; and that as Free and Independent States, they have full Power to levy War, conclude Peace, contract Alliances, establish Commerce, and to do all other Acts and Things which Independent States may of right do.—And for the support of this Declaration, with a firm reliance on the protection of Divine Providence, we mutually pledge to each other our Lives, our Fortunes and our sacred Honor.

JOHN HANCOCK.

New Hampshire
Josiah Bartlett,
Wm. Whipple,
Matthew Thornton.

Massachusetts Bay
Saml. Adams,
John Adams,
Robt. Treat Paine,
Elbridge Gerry.

Rhode Island
Step. Hopkins,
William Ellery.

Connecticut
Roger Sherman,
Sam'el Huntington,
Wm. Williams,
Oliver Wolcott.

New York
Wm. Floyd,
Phil. Livingston,
Frans. Lewis,
Lewis Morris.

New Jersey
Richd. Stockton,
Jno. Witherspoon,
Fras. Hopkinson,
John Hart,
Abra. Clark.

Pennsylvania
Robt. Morris,
Benjamin Rush,
Benja. Franklin,
John Morton,
Geo. Clymer,
Jas. Smith,
Geo. Taylor,
James Wilson,
Geo. Ross.

Delaware
Caesar Rodney,
Geo. Read,
Tho. M'Kean.

Maryland
Samuel Chase,
Wm. Paca,
Thos. Stone,
Charles Carroll *of Carrollton.*

Virginia
George Wythe,
Richard Henry Lee,
Th. Jefferson,
Benja. Harrison,
Ths. Nelson, Jr.,
Francis Lightfoot Lee,
Carter Braxton.

North Carolina
Wm. Hooper,
Joseph Hewes,
John Penn.

South Carolina
Edward Rutledge,
Thos. Heyward, Junr.,
Thomas Lynch, Junr.,
Arthur Middleton.

Georgia
Button Gwinnett,
Lyman Hall,
Geo. Walton.

Colonial America Time Line

Before the arrival of Europeans, many millions of Indians belonging to dozens of tribes lived in North America (and also in Central and South America)

About A.D. 982—Eric the Red, born in Norway, reaches Greenland during one of the first European voyages to North America

About 985—Eric the Red brings settlers from Iceland to Greenland

About 1000—Leif Ericson (Eric the Red's son) leads what is thought to be the first European expedition to mainland North America; Leif probably lands in Canada

1492—Christopher Columbus, sailing for Spain, reaches America

1497—John Cabot reaches Canada in the first English voyage to North America

1513—Ponce de León of Spain explores Florida

1519-1521—Hernando Cortés of Spain conquers Mexico

1565—St. Augustine, Florida, the first permanent European town in what is now the United States, is founded by the Spanish

1607—Jamestown, Virginia is founded, the first permanent English town in the present-day U.S.

1608—Frenchman Samuel de Champlain founds the village of Quebec, Canada

1609—Henry Hudson explores the eastern coast of present-day U.S. for the Netherlands; the Dutch then claim parts of New York, New Jersey, Delaware, and Connecticut and name the area New Netherland

1619—Virginia's House of Burgesses, America's first representative lawmaking body, is founded

1619—The first shipment of black slaves arrives in Jamestown

1620—English Pilgrims found Massachusetts' first permanent town at Plymouth

1621—Massachusetts Pilgrims and Indians hold the famous first Thanksgiving feast in colonial America

1622—Indians kill 347 settlers in Virginia

1623—Colonization of New Hampshire is begun by the English

1624—Colonization of present-day New York State is begun by the Dutch at Fort Orange (Albany)

1625—The Dutch start building New Amsterdam (now New York City)

1630—The town of Boston, Massachusetts is founded by the English Puritans

1633—Colonization of Connecticut is begun by the English

1634—Colonization of Maryland is begun by the English

1635—Boston Latin School, the colonies' first public school, is founded

1636—Harvard, the colonies' first college, is founded in Massachusetts

1636—Rhode Island colonization begins when Englishman Roger Williams founds Providence

1638—The colonies' first library is established at Harvard

1638—Delaware colonization begins when Swedish people build Fort Christina at present-day Wilmington

1640—Stephen Daye of Cambridge, Massachusetts prints *The Bay Psalm Book*, the first English-language book published in what is now the U.S.

1643—Swedish settlers begin colonizing Pennsylvania

1647—Massachusetts forms the first public school system in the colonies

1650—North Carolina is colonized by Virginia settlers in about this year

1650—Population of colonial U.S. is about 50,000

1660—New Jersey colonization is begun by the Dutch at present-day Jersey City

1670—South Carolina colonization is begun by the English near Charleston

1673—Jacques Marquette and Louis Jolliet explore the upper Mississippi River for France

1675-76—New England colonists beat Indians in King Philip's War

1682—Philadelphia, Pennsylvania is settled

1682—La Salle explores Mississippi River all the way to its mouth in Louisiana and claims the whole Mississippi Valley for France

1693—College of William and Mary is founded in Williamsburg, Virginia

1700—Colonial population is about 250,000

1704—*The Boston News-Letter*, the first successful newspaper in the colonies, is founded

1706—Benjamin Franklin is born in Boston

1732—George Washington, future first president of the United States, is born in Virginia

1733—English begin colonizing Georgia, their thirteenth colony in what is now the United States

1735—John Adams, future second president, is born in Massachusetts

1743—Thomas Jefferson, future third president, is born in Virginia

1750—Colonial population is about 1,200,000

1754—France and England begin fighting the French and Indian War over North American lands

1763—England, victorious in the war, gains Canada and most other French lands east of the Mississippi River

1764—British pass Sugar Act to gain tax money from the colonists

1765—British pass the Stamp Act, which the colonists despise; colonists then hold the Stamp Act Congress in New York City

1766—British repeal the Stamp Act

1770—British soldiers kill five Americans in the "Boston Massacre"

1773—Colonists dump British tea into Boston Harbor at the "Boston Tea Party"

1774—British close up port of Boston to punish the city for the tea party

1774—Delegates from all the colonies but Georgia meet in Philadelphia at the First Continental Congress

1775—**April 19:** Revolutionary war begins at Lexington and Concord, Massachusetts

May 10: Second Continental Congress convenes in Philadelphia

June 17: Colonists inflict heavy losses on British but lose Battle of Bunker Hill near Boston

July 3: George Washington takes command of Continental army

1776—**March 17:** Washington's troops force the British out of Boston in the first major American win of the war

May 4: Rhode Island is first colony to declare itself independent of Britain

July 4: Declaration of Independence is adopted

December 26: Washington's forces win Battle of Trenton (New Jersey)

1777—**January 3:** Americans win at Princeton, New Jersey

August 16: Americans win Battle of Bennington at New York-Vermont border

September 11: British win Battle of Brandywine Creek near Philadelphia

September 26: British capture Philadelphia

October 4: British win Battle of Germantown near Philadelphia

October 17: About 5,000 British troops surrender at Battle of Saratoga in New York

December 19: American army goes into winter quarters at Valley Forge, Pennsylvania, where more than 3,000 of them die by spring

1778—February 6: France joins the American side

July 4: American George Rogers Clark captures Kaskaskia, Illinois from the British

1779—February 23-25: George Rogers Clark captures Vincennes in Indiana

September 23: American John Paul Jones captures British ship *Serapis*

1780—May 12: British take Charleston, South Carolina

August 16: British badly defeat Americans at Camden, South Carolina

October 7: Americans defeat British at Kings Mountain, South Carolina

1781—January 17: Americans win battle at Cowpens, South Carolina

March 1: Articles of Confederation go into effect as laws of the United States

March 15: British suffer heavy losses at Battle of Guilford Courthouse in North Carolina; British then give up most of North Carolina

October 19: British army under Charles Cornwallis surrenders at Yorktown, Virginia as major revolutionary war fighting ends

1783—September 3: United States officially wins Revolution as the United States and Great Britain sign Treaty of Paris

November 25: Last British troops leave New York City

1787—On December 7, Delaware becomes the first state by approving the U.S. Constitution

1788—On June 21, New Hampshire becomes the ninth state when it approves the U.S. Constitution; with nine states having approved it, the Constitution goes into effect as the law of the United States

1789—On April 30, George Washington is inaugurated as first president of the United States

1790—On May 29, Rhode Island becomes the last of the original thirteen colonies to become a state

1791—U.S. Bill of Rights goes into effect on December 15

Bibliography

Bulla, Clyde, *A Lion to Guard Us*, New York: Crowell, 1981.
The story of English children's adventure in traveling to
Jamestown to be with their father, following the death of their
mother (useful with older, slower readers).

Campbell, Elizabeth. *The Carving on the Tree*, New York: Little,
Brown, 1968.
A true story describing the disappearance of settlers from Roanoke
Island.

Colonial Williamsburg Foundation. *A Window on Williamsburg*,
New York: Holt, Rinehart and Winston, 1983.
Photographs of present-day restoration in Williamsburg provide
information about furnishings, tools, gardens, architecture, and
other aspects of eighteenth-century life.

Fritz, Jean. *The Double Life of Pocahontas*, New York: Putnam,
1983.
A Newberry Honor Book describing the life of this famous
American Indian princess and her roles in two very different
cultures.

Fritz, Jean. *George Washington's Breakfast*, New York: Coward-
McCann, Inc., 1969.
The story of a contemporary boy in his effort to find out what
George Washington ate for breakfast. His research includes a trip
to Mount Vernon.

Knight, James, *Journey to Monticello: Traveling in Colonial
Times*, Mahwoh, New Jersey: Troll Associates, 1982.
Describes a young man's difficult journey from Massachusetts to
Virginia in 1775.

Knight, James, *Jamestown: New World Adventure*, Mahwoh, New
Jersey: Troll Associates, 1982.
Two English children are told the story of their grandfather's
experiences as one of the original Jamestown colonists.

Perl, Lyla. *Slumps, Grunts, and Snickerdoodles: What Colonial America Ate and Why*, New York: Seabury Press, 1975.
Provides an overview of colonial diets by region. Colonial recipes from the south include hush puppies and spoon bread.

Tunis, Edwin. *Shaw's Fortune*, Cleveland: World Publishing, 1966
Virginia plantation life, including the life styles of both slaves and masters, is detailed through pictures and stories. Note: this book is excellent, but no longer in print. A possible substitution by the same author is *Colonial Living* from Crowell Jr. Books, 1976.

Wagoner, Jean Brown. *Martha Washington: America's First First Lady*, New York: Bobbs-Merrill, 1983.
A classic biography from the *Childhood of Famous Americans* series, emphasizing the childhood of Martha Washington.

INDEX- *Page numbers in boldface type indicate illustrations.*

About the Author

Dennis Fradin attended Northwestern University on a partial creative scholarship and graduated in 1967. He has published stories and articles in such places as *Ingenue, The Saturday Evening Post, Scholastic, Chicago, Oui,* and *National Humane Review.* His previous books include the Young People's Stories of Our States series for Childrens Press, and *Bad Luck Tony* for Prentice—Hall. In the True book series Dennis has written about astronomy, farming, comets, archaeology, movies, space colonies, the space lab, explorers, and pioneers. He is married and the father of three children.

Photo Credits

AP/Wide World—119

The Bettmann Archive—9, 10, 13, 50, 51, 52, 54, 60 (top and bottom left), 69, 72, 79, 80 (bottom), 81, 88 (2 photos), 90, 94, 95, 96, 101, 103 (2 photos), 111, 116 (2 photos), 117, 118

© Virginia Grimes—24, 29 (right)

Historical Picture Services, Chicago— 4, 6, 8, 11, 12, 14, 18, 19 (2 photos), 20, 22 (top left), 23, 25, 27 (right), 31, 32, 33, 35, 37, 40, 44, 46, 47 (bottom), 48, 49, 53, 55, 57, 58, 59 (2 photos), 67, 68, 70 (top), 76, 77, 86, 97, 125, 138

The Library of Congress—5, 17, 27 (left), 66, 73, 84, 91 (bottom), 105, 107, 110 (bottom), 113, 121, 129 (top), 132, 134, 135, 136

North Wind Pictures Archives—7 (right), 15, 22 (top right and bottom), 26, 34, 43, 47 (top), 60 (right), 62, 63 (left), 64, 70 (1 photo, at left), 71 (2 photos), 74, 75, 80 (top), 89, 91 (top), 93, 99 (2 photos), 100, 104, 110 (top), 112, 115, 124, 126, 127, 128, 131, 133, 142

The Pierpont Morgan Library—129 (bottom)

H. Armstrong Roberts, Inc.—38, 56, 78, 83, 92, 98, 102, 106, 109, 114, 122, 123, 144

© Jim Rowan—29 (left), 61

U.S. Bureau of Engraving & Printing—140, 141

Horizon Graphics—maps

Cover and Interior Design—Horizon Graphics